Friend

within

the

Gates

the

Story

of

Nurse

Edith

Cavell

The Story of Nurse Edith Cavell

Friend

within

the

Gates

by

Elizabeth

Grey

1961

Houghton Mifflin Co.
Boston
The Riverside Press
Cambridge

ACKNOWLEDGMENTS

IT WOULD be impossible to thank individually, and adequately, the vast number of people who have personally given me help in assembling material for this book; and invidious to single out a few. To all of them, therefore, I offer my most sincere, if anonymous, gratitude for the patience, kindness and understanding with which they answered my many questions, and the time they gave up — often in the middle of a busy day — to talk to me.

For

Sister Elisabeth Wilkins, O.B.E.

who remembers, so well,

the events of the night

October 11th, 1915

AUTHOR'S NOTE

IT IS fitting that England's memorial to Nurse Edith Cavell should stand in London not far from the memorial to another steadfast fighter, Admiral Nelson. For it was Nelson who said: "England expects this day each man will do his duty."

Duty was the guiding star of Edith Cavell's life, although unlike Nelson she did not feel her duty was only to England. It was to all mankind, and it was for all suffering mankind that she fought. Because of this she laid down her own life when, by normal reckoning, it was little more than half over.

This is her story — a story which has not been easy to tell, because Edith Cavell was not a person who sought the limelight. She lived quietly, serving others and thinking little of herself. Few people really knew her, and because few knew her, the stories which are told about her are often far from accurate. In writing this book I have tried to tell the truth, in spirit if not always in precise detail, for naturally no notes were taken at the time of her conversations and thoughts, and I have, from time to time, had to deduce such things from the evidence available, and the knowledge of her character I have gained by "living with" her for more than a year.

One thing is certain; the legacy she left to the nursing profession is a great one, and the monument by which, I am sure, she would have chosen to be remembered.

"... it is not my country whose soil is desecrated and whose sacred places are laid waste. I can only feel the deep and tender pity of a friend within the gates..."

Part

I

1

THE SUN, creeping fitfully in through the dusty window, fell across the face of the little boy on the tumbled bed. He whimpered and turned his head restlessly as the bearded doctor rose from his knees and turned to the hollow-eyed woman beside him.

"Is it — is it the fever, Doctor?" the woman whispered anxiously, her eyes on the small, pale face above the tattered blanket.

The doctor nodded. "I'm afraid there's nothing more I can do for him here. He'll have to go into a hospital," he replied.

An old man shambled forward from the corner of the room and placed a hand on the woman's arm.

"Don't let them take the boy, Lizzie," he whispered. "Them 'orspitals is dreadful places. I mind when my old father died, when I were a lad — they took 'im into one o' them places and they killed 'im, they did. Those wimmin they call nurses took away 'is pillers an' sheets when they thought 'e was dyin', so's 'e'd die quicker, an' they could use 'is bed for some other poor soul. Don't let them

3

take the lad, Lizzie. They'll kill 'im too — sure as I'm standin' 'ere . . ."

"Nonsense!" The doctor turned on the old man angrily. "You've no right to say such things. The London hospitals are first rate. The boy will have every care. It's his only chance. Besides — there's the baby. If you keep the little boy here he's almost certain to catch the fever too. Then you might lose them both. I can't take the responsibility for saving them if you refuse to do as I say."

" 'E don't mean no 'arm, sir." The woman turned and frowned at the old man, shaking his hand off her arm. "It was sixty year since his old father died. He was only a lad 'imself at the time, but he's never forgotten."

"Killed 'im, they did," the old man muttered obstinately. "An' they'll kill young Johnny too, if you let 'em take 'im. You'll see."

"Things is different now, Dad. You 'eard what the doctor said." She looked imploringly at the doctor. "They are, aren't they, sir?"

"Very different. We've learned a great deal in the last sixty years, you may be sure. You have nothing to fear. The women your father spoke of belong to the past, before Miss Nightingale started her nursing service. Our nurses are well educated and well trained. They can do far more for Johnny than you can. There's a new hospital, just opened in Tooting, especially for typhoid cases: the Fountain Hospital. I'll arrange for a bed for him there."

The doctor scribbled a note on a pad of paper taken from his pocket, and handed it to Lizzie. "The ambulance will call for him tomorrow morning." He picked up the

4

shabby black bag beside the bed and moved to the door. "Don't forget what I say. Have Johnny ready by tomorrow morning without fail, or the bed will go to some other deserving child. There are half a dozen cases of fever in this street alone, and a dozen more in every street in the neighborhood. I only wish there were beds for all of them."

As the door closed behind him the old man clutched his daughter's arm again. "Don't let them take 'im, Lizzie," he implored. "You don't know what them 'orspitals is like. You 'aven't seen what I've seen."

"Stop it, Dad." Johnny's mother jerked her arm from his grasp and turned away abruptly. Frightening images danced in front of her eyes. Her father was not the only one who had told her stories of the dreaded hospitals: the brutality of the doctors; the indifference of the unskilled nurses, hired by the day or night from the streets and slums of London's East End. But all that was a long time ago now, she told herself. The doctor had said so; and everyone had heard about Miss Nightingale's nurses, who were so different from the ones her father had seen.

The little boy on the bed by the window started to whimper again. Cradling him in her arms and looking down at his waxen face her heart ached, and her mind was in a turmoil. How could she be really sure that the hospitals had changed? How could she be sure that there really would be someone — someone kind — to watch over her child and give him the care he needed?

All through the night she lay sleepless, her ears alert for the slightest sound from either of her children. Beyond the dirt-streaked window darkness had fallen and the day-

5

time sounds of the street had died away. Inside it was silent except for the muttering of the old man in his corner and the moans of the sick child. From time to time she bent over and looked at him by the light of a flickering candle. Towards morning she could see that he was worse. He lay motionless on his hard little bed, blue shadows about his lips. By the time daylight groped its way into the bare and cheerless room to touch his face, Lizzie knew that she had no choice.

With half her mind she still believed the horrifying stories her father told her. But, tired though he had been from overwork and worry, the doctor had been kind, and she trusted him. If, as he said, her boy's only chance was to go into a hospital, she must take it. This, after all, was 1895. It was not like the old days.

From the time it was fully light Lizzie moved uneasily between the bed and the window, watching anxiously for the ambulance, yet still half afraid to see it come. At last, as she crouched beside Johnny, stroking the damp hair back from his forehead, she heard the rattle of harness and the stamp of horses' hoofs below the window. One glance out was enough to show her that the time had come. Hastily wrapping the little boy in the torn blanket from his bed, she lifted him in her arms.

"Look after baby, Dad. I'm taking Johnny to the hospital," she said.

The old man hobbled to the door, barring her way. "I'm warnin' yer, Lizzie — you'll never see the boy alive again if you do. They only want us poor folks for experimentin' on. They'll cut Johnny up, for sure . . ."

With a sob, Lizzie pushed him aside and snatched open the rickety door of the one room she, and her father, and her two children called "home," and hurried down the stairs.

Outside, the horse-drawn ambulance was standing. The driver and attendant were opening the big double doors at the back. All up and down the street Lizzie could see pale, frightened faces at windows and half-open doors.

"You've — you've come for Johnny, haven't you?" she whispered to the burly, red-faced driver.

"That's right, M'm. This the little nipper? 'Ere — give 'im ter me."

Lizzie shrank back, holding Johnny more tightly.

"Want to take 'im in yerself, do you? Well, that's all right. 'Op in."

Lizzie climbed up the step behind the ambulance and crept inside. It was spartanly furnished with two or three stretchers. She sat down gingerly on one of them. The attendant swung in behind her and the driver slammed the big doors. With a jerk and a jingle of harness, they rattled off over the cobbles.

The journey was a long one. The new hospital had been built on the outskirts of southwest London, several miles from the seething, sprawling mass of factories and tenements where Lizzie had lived all her life. Suddenly the ambulance swung round a corner, startling into wakefulness the attendant, who had been sleeping in his corner with his mouth open.

" 'Ere we are, Ma," he said, yawning. "Won't be long now before we 'ave the little feller in bed, all tucked up

7

cozy." He leaned forward and moved the blanket from Johnny's face. "Terrible thing, this fever," he added solemnly. "Thousands of cases we've 'ad these last weeks. Nusses is run off their feet."

"They'll — they'll be kind to Johnny, won't they?" Lizzie pleaded timidly.

"Kind? O' course they will. Wunnerful, they are. Never seem to sleep, most of 'em. Don't know 'ow they keeps goin'. Yet kind? More like angels than wimmin, some of 'em."

The big doors at the back of the ambulance opened and the driver lowered the step. Lizzie climbed down and looked round. The ambulance was standing on a broad path beside a low building of unpainted corrugated iron. Other, similar buildings were scattered over a wide area, with paths running between them. Everything looked rawly new; corrugated iron, window frames and doors stood about in untidy heaps; the paths were unfinished — some of them little more than rutted tracks. Used as she was to the big, old hospitals of London; soot-blackened brick barracks with serried rows of windows, which looked as if they had existed since the beginning of time, Lizzie felt bewildered, and dubious. Surely this couldn't be the place?

The attendant was touching her arm. "If you give me the doctor's note, I'll give it to Nurse Cavell — then you can take the nipper straight into the ward," he said kindly. Lizzie handed over the precious piece of paper and the attendant disappeared. Lizzie looked round again at this new, strange place which looked so unlike a hospital to her. Men in dark coats and women in crisp, starched aprons hurried along the paths between the hutments, their faces set and preoccupied. There was a sense of urgency about all of them, and they looked tired and strained. How could they, remote and busy as they were, really care about a little boy who meant nothing to them?

There was a sound of quick, light footsteps behind her and she turned. The woman approaching her was small, and very slender. Her brown hair was brushed back from her face and almost concealed by the white cap she wore. But it was her eyes which riveted Lizzie's attention. Brilliantly clear and gray, they seemed to look straight into her mind and heart, and to understand what they saw there. In spite of her fears of a few minutes earlier, she found herself willing to surrender Johnny for the first time since he became ill. And as she put him into the nurse's arms, it seemed that the burden had been taken not only from her arms but from her heart.

"Poor little soul," the nurse said, so softly that Lizzie hardly heard the words. Then she looked up. "I'm Nurse Cavell," she went on. "Come with me — we'll put him straight into bed."

She turned and led the way through a door into a huge room, lined on both sides with close-set beds. The floor was polished and everything was clean and tidy. There was a tangy smell in the air which caught Lizzie by the throat, but it was not unpleasant. She followed the nurse across to an empty bed and watched her fold back the blankets and then tuck Johnny expertly between them.

"Miss . . . they won't . . . they won't . . . cut 'im

9

open, will they?" she whispered in a frightened voice.

Nurse Cavell looked up sharply. "Good gracious, no — what put such an idea into your head?" Seeing the expression on Lizzie's face she went on more gently: "He won't need an operation. Just careful nursing." She touched Lizzie's arm fleetingly. "Try not to worry. We'll do our best for your little boy."

Lizzie felt the tears rising in her throat. "He won't — die, will he Miss?"

Nurse Cavell looked grave. "Not if we can help it." She stiffened her already straight back. "He's very poorly — you know that, don't you? But if nursing can save him, he'll get well, I promise."

The little room in which Lizzie lived seemed almost empty that night, without Johnny lying beside her. As she closed her heavy-lidded eyes she could see the imprint of his white, pinched face against the clean hospital pillow. It had seemed almost lifeless when she took a last, lingering look before she left the ward; but strangely enough she had left the hospital with a quiet mind, hugging to herself the memory of the nurse's tender smile as she bent over the iron cot, her sensitive hands busy and her tired face serene. There was something about the slight, gray-eyed woman who had taken Johnny from her arms that gave her new hope. If anyone could save him, Lizzie thought to herself, it would be Nurse Cavell. And Lizzie was right.

2

ALTHOUGH Lizzie did not know it, Edith Cavell had at that time been nursing for only a very few weeks. But even in so short a time she had come to realize that nursing was the job she had been looking for all her life; the work for which life had been preparing her ever since the day, thirty years earlier, when she had first opened her wide gray eyes onto an English landscape.

There were few people about on that cold December day in 1865. The wind, whipping the gray clouds to a froth like dirty soapsuds, scudded across the flat Norfolk country-side over the leafless hedges and trees. It flattened the grass on Swardeston Common and riffled the water of the village pond until it glittered like broken glass.

The brick house standing alone in the hollow on the edge of the Common looked snug and sleepy, with its windows closed and its sheltering trees dipping their branches protectively over its roof. It gave no outward sign that an event of great family importance was taking place inside. A farm laborer, plodding past the gate with his horse, glanced once at the closed door, and went on his way. But,

11

in that mysterious fashion in which news spreads in the country, by evening everyone in the tiny village knew . . .

"A daughter!" The village women nodded and smiled at each other over the fences and hedges which separated their gardens. "That'll be nice for Vicar's wife. Company for her, like, in that grand new house Vicar's building by the church." They glanced with something like awe across the Common to where the walls of the big new brick vicarage were rising beside the old flint church. Then they smiled at each other, pleased at the thought of the new baby who had been born that day in their village.

"What'll they call her?" they wondered as they pulled their shawls more closely round their shoulders against the winter wind.

They called her Edith Louisa; Louisa for her gentle, warmhearted mother, wife of the Reverend Frederick Cavell, the stern, bearded and often formidable vicar of Swardeston parish. And as she grew from babyhood the villagers could see that she had inherited more than her mother's name; she had the same warm smile, soft brown hair and clear gray eyes; the same swiftness to help when a villager was in difficulties and kindly understanding of their small troubles.

But there was something of her father in her, too. The eyes were serious, and the sensitive mouth was firm at the corners.

Life was not easy in the big vicarage to which Edith and her parents moved from the cozy house on the Common while she was still very small. There was not much money, and what there was had to be shared. First Edith, and later her sisters Florence and Lilian, and her brother Jack, were taught by their father that their duty was always to others less fortunate than themselves. It was not a hard lesson to learn in England in the 1860's and '70's. Poor though the vicarage family was, the villagers were poorer still, and almost before she could walk Edith was first taken, then sent, on errands of mercy — carrying food to hungry families.

It was difficult, sometimes, to carry the hot food along the dusty lanes in a basin which almost burned her fingers, knowing that her own food was cooling on the table in the vicarage dining room, and that by the time she returned from her long walk it would be disagreeably cold and un-appetizing on her plate. It was hard to wait patiently as the hungry families thanked her, with tears in their eyes, for her father's generosity, while all the time the savory scent of the meat in the basins they clutched tantalized her nose and set her mouth watering with hunger.

But if she ever thought of rebellion, she gave no sign. Deep in her heart she understood her father's urge to help the helpless, feed the hungry and bring comfort to those in distress, even though her father's way of doing these things was not always the way she herself would have chosen. For him, duty to his fellows was a burden laid on him by the hand of God, whereas for her, as for her mother, to help those in distress was something much more personal; something as necessary to her as it was to those she helped: a practical joy, not a cross to be borne with fortitude.

Entertainments were few in the English countryside at

the turn of the century, and the Cavell children learned to make the most of the simple pleasures which lay close at hand. Edith soon discovered the joys of drawing and painting the country scenes around her home, and when her younger sisters and brother were too small to read, she drew pictures for them, as well as for her own amusement. Her skill grew quickly, and with it her pleasure increased. But even this talent she turned to use for others in a most practical manner.

She knew that for some time her parents had been worried about the lack of a Sunday school in the village. At first she listened idly as they discussed the problem; but gradually the feeling grew in her that just to talk about a problem was not enough, and so she sat down quietly one day at the big table where she and her sisters did their lessons, and she wrote a letter to the Bishop of Norwich, the nearby town, asking for his help.

Luckily the Bishop was an understanding man. Though he might so easily have dismissed the childish letter as unimportant, he wrote back kindly, explaining that such a school would cost money, and that although he was unable to supply all that was necessary, if the village could raise part of it he would see what he could do to provide the rest.

Greatly excited, Edith showed the letter to her parents, who were naturally a little shocked by their daughter's innocent daring in writing to such an eminent man. But mingled with their disapproval there must have been pride in her earnest desire to help in the parish work. Perhaps they were even a little amused — and more than a little

14

skeptical about her ability to raise even a few shillings in such a poor district. But once permission was given, Edith was undeterred by their lack of encouragement. There was not much, it was true, that she could do to raise money — but there were her paintings. Often visitors to the house had praised little sketches she had drawn and painted on Christmas cards and invitations to church functions. Perhaps people would be glad to pay a few pennies — even shillings — to buy one of them in such a good cause?

Industriously she set to work with pencils and paintbox. Dozens of birthday, Christmas and Easter cards took shape and color under her busy fingers. Gradually the family began to be impressed by her determination. Her small sisters, too young and unskilled to do the actual painting, were set to work cutting out the cards and cleaning the dirty brushes. Even her parents, touched by her enthusiasm, played their part by addressing envelopes and writing little notes of explanation to friends and acquaintances round the countryside. Little Jack trotted busily to and from the village postbox with bundles of envelopes in his chubby hands.

And so, by the end of the year the pennies and shillings had grown into pounds, and a second letter was written to the Bishop of Norwich, reminding him of his promise. Probably he was more than a little taken aback to find that his suggestion had borne such substantial fruit, but he kept his word; the money was provided, and building began. A secondhand piano and some chairs were bought, and the village of Swardeston had its Sunday school at last — thanks to twelve-year-old Edith Cavell.

Edith was growing, and learning, fast now. At first, because there was no money available to send her away to school, and there was no suitable school near at hand, she learned all her lessons at home. It was a quiet, withdrawn, narrow life, filled with restrictions, and without much fun, but Edith was not unhappy. She adored her mother and, because she understood him in her childish way, she loved her solemn father too. She had her two small sisters and baby brother to play with and for her the changing seasons were full of excitement and wonder.

There were, too, occasional seaside holidays with her cousin Eddy, who became her lifelong friend; to whom when she was beginning to grow up she confided her dreams and hopes. To whom she said: "Some day, somehow, I am going to do something useful . . . I don't know what it will be, but it must be something for *people*. They are, most of them, so helpless, so hurt and so unhappy."

Her parents, recognizing her quickly growing intelligence, realized that she should have more opportunity to learn than they could provide, and at last enough money was found to send her away for a few years to school.

Life at Laurel Court, Miss Gibson's School for Young Ladies in Peterborough, was not very different from the life Edith had known at home. Like Norwich, Peterborough was a cathedral city; its life revolved round the big church whose bells rang out over the sleepy streets, and it was only once a week, on market day, that the town woke from its placid doze.

Edith's routine of school lessons, church services and

simple pleasures continued almost exactly as it had done at home. But every day new paths were opening out for her lively, inquiring mind to explore; and new people — girls of her own age as well as the teachers — helped her to widen her horizons beyond the tiny village where she had spent so much of her life.

She loved learning new things; and especially she loved languages. She had a gift for them and now, for the first time, she had the opportunity to learn to speak French fluently. She reached for it eagerly. She felt stirring in her too the first conscious desire to help others to learn, to widen other people's horizons and enrich their lives as her own was being enriched.

But how? Finding the sort of job she wanted, in 1884, was not the simple matter it is today. "I want to do something for people," she was to say to her cousin Eddy a few years later, but at nineteen it was not so easy to find the way. If she had been rich she could have taken a ladylike interest in a hospital or orphanage. But money was still short at home — she had to earn a living; and in any case, that was not what she wanted. She wanted to *do* something, not talk about it . . . as she had "done something" about the much needed Sunday school six years earlier.

Becoming a governess, at Miss Gibson's suggestion, was not a satisfactory solution, but at least it meant she would have children to love and care for again. Her own brother and sisters were growing up now; they no longer needed her to read stories to them, or to draw little pictures for their amusement, and she missed the eager, coaxing cries of "Tell us a story, Edith," or "Please draw us a picture . . ." and the feel of small, tousled heads against her shoulder as she read or drew for an admiring audience.

No, being a governess might not be the complete solution to her dreams, but it was perhaps a beginning. And there seemed at the time nothing else.

She set off for her first job with Miss Gibson's letter of recommendation in her pocket; her skirts an inch or so longer and her brown hair swept up neatly, determined that even if this was not the job she would have chosen, she would at least do it well. And, like everything else she undertook, she made a success of it. The parents of the children she taught wrote gratefully to Miss Gibson, reporting on the progress their children made under her care. The children loved her too, and for a time it seemed that perhaps this was her niche in life after all.

The years slipped by, unmarked by any great event until one day Miss Gibson wrote a letter which was to change Edith's life completely, and forever.

Two Belgian friends of hers, Monsieur and Madame François, wanted an English governess for their four children: three daughters and a son. Would Edith like to accept the post? Miss Gibson felt sure that with her good knowledge of French and her experience as a governess in England she would find the work pleasant and not unduly difficult. And of course it would be a wonderful experience for her.

In her small room in the country house where she was employed at the time, Edith sat with the letter in her hand, dazed by the unexpectedness of the suggestion. The six years of teaching which lay behind her had slipped away with the smooth, unruffled calm of a river flowing quietly through the gentle countryside which surrounded her. Now it seemed that the river was to meet the turbulent sea of the great world outside — and she could go with it, if she chose . . .

Her thoughts began to whirl excitedly. To travel abroad . . . to see new places, meet new people; to live in one of the gayest capitals of Europe . . . it all seemed like an impossible dream. Under her window childish voices were arguing over the possession of a ball. Far away in the kitchen regions the familiar clatter of pots and pans announced the preparations for lunch. It seemed extraordinary that everything should be going on in just the same way when here, in her hand, she held the key to a wonderful, exciting future.

A few weeks later she packed her trunks, said farewell to her English charges, and traveled down to the Channel coast. The sea was calm and unruffled, the sky an unclouded blue. It was a perfect day for starting a new life, in a new country, among new people.

But the new life, when she reached it, was not without its problems. It was a puzzling new world at times, among people different from any she had ever known before. The Belgians were so much gayer and more lighthearted than the sober people among whom Edith had grown up. She was shocked, sometimes, by their careless attitude to some of the things she had been taught to hold in reverence.

Shortly after her arrival in Brussels Madame François called her into the drawing room.

"The parlor maid will be out this afternoon, Miss

Cavell," she said. "Would you please answer the door to any callers? Oh, and please tell them that I shall be out myself."

As she turned to leave the room, Edith paused. "Will you be back in time for dinner, Madame François?" she asked politely.

Madame François laughed. "Oh, I shall not really be out," she explained. "But I shall be busy, and do not wish to see anyone this afternoon."

Strictly brought up as she had been in a little English village, it was Edith's first encounter with this social "white lie," so often used and easily understood in city life. Indignantly she drew herself up to her full five feet three inches.

"But Madame, I could not say you were out if you were not," she protested firmly.

Madame's eyebrows shot up in surprise. "Nonsense, Miss Cavell. Everyone understands. It is the usual thing to say," she replied mildly, and with some amusement. But Edith was not to be shaken. Truth, to her, was sacred. Either a thing was so, or it was not — there could be no compromise.

At last Madame François shrugged her shoulders. The English were odd people. But there, it was a small thing, not worth arguing about. Miss Cavell was so good with the children — it was worth putting up with her eccentricities to know that they were well cared for. With another shrug she turned back to the letters on her writing table, and Edith left the room, victor in the small domestic battle.

It was not the only time her high principles caused surprise and embarrassment to her employers. One evening at dinner, which Edith shared with her employers, Monsieur François spoke scathingly of Queen Victoria, denouncing her narrow, prudish outlook. Edith listened in silence at first, her lips pressed firmly together; but at last, rising from her seat, her eyes flashing, she said in a voice which shook slightly: "Monsieur, I cannot listen to such criticism of my Queen," and she left the room, her meal half finished on her plate.

For a moment after she had gone there was a surprised silence, then Monsieur François shrugged his shoulders, as his wife had done on an earlier occasion. "Ah — the English!" he commented, rolling his eyes and waving his hands. "How can one ever understand them?"

But if Monsieur and Madame François sometimes found their quiet-spoken, uncompromising governess disconcerting, the children had no such difficulties. To them, their dear Miss Cavell was the center of their small world — always ready with a word of comfort and a soothing touch when a knee or elbow was grazed in play — always full of fascinating stories about her own childhood in faraway Swardeston with the sisters and brother they had never seen. Always willing to draw a picture or write a little poem to make a dull lesson interesting.

They even learned to accept punishment when they were naughty without a feeling of injustice. Miss Cavell was not like other grownups. She explained just why certain things were wrong, and you knew that if she said a thing was wrong, she would not punish you for it and then later do it herself, as some grownups did.

If the children were learning from Edith, she was learning too; from them and from their parents. Learning not only to speak more perfect French, but to understand the differences between herself and these sometimes flippant people who had grown up in such a different atmosphere from the one she had always known. In spite of their difference she grew to love them; their gaiety and warmheartedness and their quick appreciation of beauty. Their standards of conduct would never be hers, but during her five years with the François family she learned tolerance of their ways. They were, after all, *people* — and all people had good in them.

She learned to love Belgium, too; the great, bell-haunted squares and narrow streets of Brussels, and the woods and fields which surrounded it. It became her "second country" — second only to the quiet English countryside where she had been born.

But all was not well at home. Her father was growing older, and when she had been with the François family for just five years a letter came one autumn morning bearing bad news. Her father was ill — very ill — and her mother needed help.

Eight-year-old Evelyn and thirteen-year-old Hélène cried, and clung to her when she said goodbye. Even George and Marguerite, almost grown up now at seventeen and eighteen, forgot their new dignity and flung their arms round her before she left. Her last sight of them was blurred by tears as she leaned out of the window of the station cab behind the clip-clopping old horse which pulled

22

her farther and farther away from the little cluster of waving figures.

Sighing, she sat back against the cushioned seat when the corner was at last turned. Behind her lay five of the happiest years of her life. What lay ahead? Would she, now that she was stepping out of the cab and following the porter with her luggage into the gloomy Brussels railway station, ever see her beloved Belgium again?

At home, the Vicarage seemed quieter than ever. The rollicking carillons of Brussels seemed very far away as Edith listened on Sundays to the sound of the single little bell in the old flint tower of Swardeston Church, stealing across the Common to call the villagers to evening service. She missed the voices of "her" children; though she realized that soon her work for them would have been over anyway — soon they would be going out into the world, the better for her love and guidance, but the need for her care and companionship done.

Here at home were people who needed her more. Her father, who had always been so busy and active helping others, lay uncharacteristically still and helpless. Her mother's face was drawn with anxiety and fatigue.

Edith's hands, which had gently tended the François children when they were hurt, had the same gentleness as they tended her father, and she brought comfort to her worried mother as she had to Hélène and Evelyn when childish griefs overwhelmed them.

At the beginning, this time at home seemed like a little backwater into which she had drifted at the age of twenty-

23

nine, but as the months went by, the future began to look clearer. Happy as her years in Brussels had been, she had known in her heart that being a governess was not her real life work. It had not been easy to see what that work was, but gradually, as she eased her father's pain, reassured her mother and watched over the troubled household, the big question mark which hung over her future drifted away.

By the late autumn of 1895 she knew she would be a nurse — a hospital nurse. Bringing her father back almost from the brink of death had been a rewarding and satisfying experience, not only because he was her father, but simply because he was someone who needed her and whom she could help. And yet her father already had so much: the love and devotion of her mother; the good country air of Norfolk to speed his recovery; the kindly ministrations of the doctor who had been for so many years not only their doctor, but a close friend of the family.

What of those others — those thousands upon thousands of others, who by comparison had nothing? There were people, she knew, living in the slums of the big cities whose lives were a constant battle against dirt and disease; who only saw the sunlight as a golden haze, far above the chimney pots, through a permanent cloud of smoke and dust; who had no one to love and care for them when illness struck them down. Surely, these people needed her even more.

3

It was characteristic of Edith Cavell that she should choose to start her nursing career in the hastily erected emergency Fountain Hospital — built to house the overflow of typhoid victims from the squalid slums of London. This was the place where she felt she was most urgently needed — and that was enough for her. And the three months she spent in its flimsy wards, among its half-finished pathways, its "temporary" surgeries and storerooms, served to convince her, if she had ever doubted it, that here, at last, was the job she had been looking for throughout most of her thirty years; the job towards which she had been groping when she told her cousin Eddy: ". . . it must be something for *people*. They are, most of them, so helpless, so hurt and so unhappy."

But she could not stay there long. The rules laid down that to become a fully trained nurse she must spend at least one year at a general hospital where formal training was given. There were several teaching hospitals for her to choose from. Perhaps it was a kindly fate which led her to choose the London Hospital. Or perhaps she heard the other nurses at the Fountain talking about the hospital which had been famous in the East End for more than a hundred and fifty years already. If so, she would certainly have heard them talking about its Matron, Miss Lückes who, in her way, was almost as much of a legend as the hospital itself.

Even so, as she sat in her tiny, boxlike room at the Fountain carefully filling in the form of application which was to set her feet on the road from which she was never to deviate for the rest of her days, Edith could hardly have realized that it would soon be in the hands of the woman who, after her mother and Miss Gibson, was to be the greatest influence in her life.

In many ways, Edith chose her moment well to enter the London Hospital. Here, as in so many other places, the second half of the nineteenth century was a time of great reform. Until Miss Lückes's appointment, nineteen years earlier, conditions for the nursing staff had hardly changed from those of the "bad old days." Nurses still slept, turn and turn about, in the stuffy little attics; bathrooms were almost nonexistent. Uniform was scanty and only one meal a day was provided — an allowance of bread and tea was made for the other meals, which had to be snatched when and where the nurses could find the time, the place and the money to obtain them. Hours were long, and off-duty time too brief for it to give real rest and refreshment.

Into this daunting sea of problems and obstacles, Miss Lückes had swept like a galleon under full sail. Committees, hitherto well satisfied with the running of the hospital, found themselves under fire from all her not inconsiderable guns. Although the comfort and welfare of patients was always her first concern, she fought no less fiercely for her nurses. First of all she demanded a proper training school; then that living conditions and feeding arrangements for the nurses should be improved; adequate uniform provided; better meals, and country holidays for sick and tired nurses; a proper pension scheme for them when they retired after their long years of service.

There seemed no end to her demands and the Committee, at first bewildered that anyone so young and pretty (for Miss Lückes was only twenty-six at the time of her appointment) should also be so practical, hard-headed and hard-hitting, began gradually to yield to her importunities, especially when experience proved that well-trained and well-equipped nurses meant better cared for and more quickly recovered patients.

By 1896, the year that Edith entered the London, Miss Lückes had been joined by an ally: Viscount Knutsford, an energetic man of affairs, was appointed Chairman of the hospital. He was a man after Matron's own heart. Impatient of inefficiency, in equipment as well as in those who used it, he swept the cobwebs of long-standing practice out of the dark and dusty corners and, cheered on by the delighted Miss Lückes, campaigned for more up-to-date methods throughout the hospital.

Between them, they transformed the London from what was little more than a "pest house," and it was into this stimulating atmosphere of progress that Edith stepped one memorable summer afternoon. She left the heat and glare,

27

the dust and stench of the Whitechapel streets, where the battle of life was a grim one indeed, and entered the long corridors and dimly lit wards which were another battle-ground — against the death and disease those streets engendered.

She paused on the edge of the pavement before crossing the road to the hospital and looked up at the rows of windows, set in soot-blackened brick, which frowned down upon her. Unlike the Fountain, this, she could see, was no hastily erected emergency hospital of temporary buildings. Four-square and solid, the London loomed over the bustling highway which cut through the heart of Whitechapel as if it had grown out of the sooty cobblestones themselves until, a vast, immovable rock, it towered above the swarming tenements and narrow alleys of East London.

All about her, costers bawled their wares behind the barrows lining the roadway. Shawled and shabby women, clutching tattered shopping bags, haggled over prices and counted out their ha'pennies with jealous care. After the peace and quiet of Norfolk, the dignified luxury and gaiety of Brussels and the bright modernity of the Fountain, Whitechapel seemed like another, a nightmarish world into which she had strayed by accident.

Strange smells assailed her nostrils. Wraithlike figures brushed against her, whining plaintively and stretching out dirty, clawlike hands for alms. In a nearby doorway two children crouched — one as still and pale as death itself, the other listlessly picking at the sores which covered its face.

Her heart contracted with pity. At the Fountain, and

even in Swardeston, she had often been hurt and stirred to the depths of her being by the results of poverty and ignorance; but she had seen nothing quite like this. Here, all about her — in the heart of one of the greatest capital cities in the world — were hurt, helpless and unhappy people crying out for her help.

But only a few yards away stood the vast building in which she was going to be able to help them. With a lift of the heart she looked again at the intimidating, fortress-like façade across the road, then, accepting the silent challenge it threw out above the clatter of horses' hoofs and the rattle of wheels, she crossed the road and climbed the shallow flight of steps. The door swung to behind her. At last, her real life had begun.

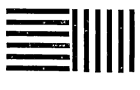

4

THERE FOLLOWED for Edith five long years of work and study; of long hours and very little financial reward; of restrictions, self-discipline and the gradual acceptance of the horror of suffering and death. Many years later, she was to say: "I have seen death so often it is not strange or fearful to me . . ." It was at the London that she first came face to face with death in its more terrible forms, and was to recognize that it could also bring peace and release from suffering, as often as it brought sadness.

They were not, for all that, unhappy years. She was conscious always that she was doing the work for which she was most fitted; learning each day to do it more skillfully. Her pile of well-thumbed notebooks grew, as did the deftness of her hands.

If she ever paused, wistfully, and leaned her aching head against the smeared glass of the little window of her cell-like room and gazed down at the seething streets below, it was to remember the lanes of Norfolk; powdered over with summer dust, and the song of the birds in the vicarage garden. She was still, at heart, a countrywoman and missed the quiet pleasures of village life. Whenever possible she spent her scanty off-duty time in the country round about London with one of the other nurses with whom she made friends.

She was still shy, and to most of the other nurses, busy about their unending duties, a remote, withdrawn figure about whom they scarcely gave a second thought; but Evaline Dickenson, more perceptive than most perhaps, saw beneath the reserved surface of the dedicated nurse to the warm, compassionate woman whose gentle hands and quiet voice brought comfort to so many patients. It was she who shared the long walks, the sunny afternoons spent sketching, the dreams and hopes for the future.

For Evaline, the dreams of wider service changed after a few years to a more personal dream of happiness, and after she married and went to live with her husband in Ireland, Edith was once more solitary. For her there never seems to have been even a fleeting dream of marriage, and motherhood. From the first, all mankind were her children and though she shared, just for a little, in the cheerful bustle of preparation for her friend's wedding, it never occurred to her that such personal happiness should be hers.

She did not forget her own family, though. Whenever she could get away from London she traveled to Norfolk to visit her parents, and her old friends in Swardeston. These visits were a life line — a reminder that life was not all squalor and sickness. Here still were trees, cloud-flecked sky, larks still singing for pure joy over the Common. Still, the greatest joy of all, a dog to bring her sticks to throw as she walked by the village pond.

31

Her parents did not share her love of animals, and there was never a family pet, but she "borrowed" dogs of all shapes and sizes from friends and neighbors, and was rarely without one on her walks and visits during her brief spells in the country.

In time Edith came to love and revere the dour, gray building in which she learned the professional skills which were so necessary for her chosen work. To some, the London might seem a grim, forbidding place, but Edith was to remember it always with pride and affection — a pride and affection which was to stiffen her will in times of trial and set her standards firm and high.

She remembered, perhaps best of all, Mellish Ward, where she spent so much of her duty time. Long, narrow, overshadowed by the walls of other buildings so that the sun which shone over Swardeston Common never reached its wooden floor, it was nevertheless, a cheerful place. During the winter a bright coal fire danced in the green-tiled fireplace and gas jets flared along the walls. Blue and white checked curtains hung on each side of the narrow iron beds and across the foot of each a scarlet flannel cape (worn by the patient during the doctors' rounds) was smoothly spread. As the nurses, in their long mauve dresses and starched white caps and aprons, moved briskly about, it was as warm and cheerful a sight as many of the slum-dwelling patients had ever seen. Not, perhaps, as hygienic as a present-day hospital ward, but for all that a homely and comforting place for the sick.

And over it all, as over the whole hospital, reigned the

sternly benevolent figure of Matron Lückes; intolerant of slackness, but ever ready to understand and interest herself in the problems and difficulties of patients and nurses alike.

From her Edith was learning much more than the technicalities of nursing. She was, in fact, learning that technical knowledge was not enough. Nursing, even more than doctoring, needed the personal touch. Matron maintained it not only with the patients, but with her individual nurses. Not everyone enjoyed the Tuesday evening "At Homes" she held every week; for a raw young probationer, guiltily conscious of a broken bedpan or a torn sheet, they could be an ordeal. Matron had a reputation for knowing all that went on in every department of the hospital — of having X-ray eyes which could see through walls and round corners, and a tendency to discuss even quite small, unimportant things during those two-hour meetings.

But they soon learned that she was just as likely to remember, and praise, a thoughtful act as censure a careless one, and just as likely to refer to some quite personal matter of interest only to herself and the nurse concerned. So that the meetings, formidable though they could be to those with uneasy consciences, not only strengthened discipline, but deepened the feeling among the nurses that Matron, in spite of her many preoccupations, was personally interested in each one of them.

Edith was to remember those Tuesday evenings. Ten years later she herself, immersed in the many administrative duties of a growing hospital, was to follow Miss Lückes's example in this as in so many other ways.

33

5

DURING her second year of nursing Edith tasted, through
a strange echo of her earliest nursing days, her first experience of responsibility and authority. An epidemic of
typhoid fever had broken out in the rapidly expanding
town of Maidstone, in Kent, where the sudden increase in
population had speedily outgrown the town's inadequate
sewerage system. It spread with terrifying speed until the
local hospital staff were incapable of dealing with it.
Schools and parish halls were turned into hastily impro-
vised nursing centers; soup kitchens were set up to help
feed stricken families suddenly deprived of their bread-
winners.

An S O S was sent out to the big London hospitals.
Among others the London answered the call, and with a
handful of her colleagues Edith was sent down to Kent
to help organize the near-chaotic situation.

It was the sort of job which brought out the best in her.
Not only was she nursing the sick and fighting a battle
against disease, but she was doing so in a situation which
demanded every ounce of ingenuity, improvisation and

organizing ability. Nurses who could work only to a set routine in an orderly hospital ward would have been useless. Because of the overcrowding of hospitals and emergency centers many of the cases had to be nursed in tents, or in their own homes, and Edith found herself remembering, and being thankful for, her early training in visiting the sick and poor of her own village. Gently reared though she was, it was not difficult for her to make herself at home in the humblest cottage, and her patients quickly came to look on her as a friend.

When the time came for her to leave the London — as unobtrusively as she had entered it, though wiser and more skilled — this experience proved to be invaluable to her; for it was then that she took up her first post of real authority, as night superintendent in the North St. Pancras Infirmary — a hospital very different from the one where she had done her training.

In Edith's day hospitals in Britain were of two different kinds; the "voluntary hospital" — that is, a hospital supported entirely by voluntary contributions from the more generous-minded citizens, and the Poor Law institutions administered by local authority Boards of Guardians.

From the point of view of the doctors and nurses the big difference between the two was that whereas the voluntary hospitals were at liberty to — and sometimes did — refuse admission to patients they felt were too dirty and verminous to be acceptable in the wards, the Poor Law institutions had no such privilege. They were bound by law to admit every case which was brought to their doors.

The London, a voluntary hospital, had been a tough

enough school for someone who had led a sheltered life for her first thirty years, but the North St. Pancras — a Poor Law Institute — was to open Edith's eyes even wider to the misery of life in the heart of a vast city.

The hospital itself was modern for its time. It stood on a hillside overlooking the slum area it served, but apart from it. The buildings were surrounded by gardens, which in their turn were bounded by a private park where the nurses were at liberty to wander during their off-duty time. Edith's room was small, and high up beneath the eaves overlooking the park. From its tall windows she could see trees and grass, and above the clatter of the hospital, hear birdsong on a summer's morning when her turn of duty was over. Sitting there with the breeze cool on her forehead after a night in the stuffy wards it was almost possible, for the first time since she had arrived in London, to believe that she was back in the country again, though she had only to open her door to see through the corridor windows the thick pall of smoke which lay over the huddle of roofs and chimneys, and to be reminded that Norfolk was very far away indeed.

For it was from under that huddle of chimneys and roofs that her new patients came: people just as poverty-stricken and pathetic as those she had left behind in Whitechapel. It wrung her heart, sometimes, to send a patient, still white-faced and shaky, back to the sunless streets and damp, depressing hovel which was the only place he knew as "home"; or to turn out a fever-weakened child from his hospital bed when she knew his only refuge was a tenement room, already overcrowded and filthy.

37

Remembering her visits to the typhoid-stricken homes of Maidstone, the gratitude of the bewildered townsfolk for the gifts of bread and secondhand clothes and help in nursing their families, she began, tentatively, to make little sorties beyond the hospital walls, following her patients back into the places where disease had its roots.

In someone less used to the consequences of poverty, and less accustomed to visiting the needy in their homes, it would have been a courageous and harrowing decision to make, but Edith was far past the need for courage in taking such a step. It was a job she felt needed doing, and she did it without fuss.

At first frightened and suspicious of the visits from someone in authority at the hospital on the hill, the slum dwellers gradually lost their reserve. They began to realize that "Nurse's" visits were kindly meant; that her lessons in simple sickroom cookery (a blessed legacy from Matron Lückes) and suggestions for keeping the children cleaner and warmer were not critically meant, but made with full appreciation of their difficulties.

Edith became, more and more, a familiar and welcome figure among the streets and alleys, her blue-clad figure a signal for the children to turn out in their dozens and trot beside her, clutching at her hand with grubby little paws and fighting for the privilege of walking beside her. She moved as safely here, among the sinister shadows, as she did along the dim corridors and night-darkened wards of the hospital.

Perhaps the immunity she bought for herself with her kindness made her careless. For not all of London was as safe as she had made her own particular corner of it, as she discovered one summer's evening when she was returning from one of her hard-earned days in the country.

She wrote about her experience in her first letter to her old matron.

St. Pancras
2nd July 1901

My dear Matron,

You will have heard how unfortunately I was placed on Sunday night, when after coming back from a day in the country I was robbed of my purse and had no means of returning here. If I had had anywhere else to go I would not have returned to the hospital to trespass on the time of the night sisters . . . but it was too wet to walk, and there seemed nothing else to do . . .

It was the first time after leaving the London that she turned back to Miss Lückes for help. But there were to be many, many more times. Over the remaining years of her life she was to share most of her worries, as well as her triumphs, with the woman who had shaped her nursing life; and she was never to cease expressing her gratitude to the Matron, and the Hospital, for all they had done for her.

Her second letter to Miss Lückes was a much happier one. Two years after her encounter with the London footpad she wrote jubilantly:

You will, I think, be pleased to hear that I was elected yesterday to the post of Assistant Matron at Shoreditch Infirmary. I am glad to have obtained some day work after my three years of night duty

— also I hope the position will prove a help for the
future, and the salary is larger than the one I am
receiving at present.

I am glad to know I shall have much supervision
of the wards under Miss Inglis, and be able to teach
the probationers and improve their work. I shall
also have charge of the linen room and have to
overlook the laundry. It will be a new experience,
and I hope to learn much from it . . .

To learn, and to teach — the happiest combination of
activities for Edith Cavell. Life was to go on teaching her
its lessons, many of them bitter ones, to the end of her
days; and she was to pass on what she learned with a skill
born of innate intelligence and the magnificent training
she had received, first at the hands of her parents, and later
at her beloved London Hospital.

Only one thing she was destined never to learn — to
take life lightly; to laugh at the serio-comic incidents with
which hospital life is filled. From the beginning, apart
from the short interlude with the François family in Brussels, life had most often shown her its darker side, and the
shadow rested in her grave gray eyes.

Had she been capable of it, she might have learned the
art of laughter from Joan Inglis, Matron of the Shoreditch
Infirmary, whose own eyes more often danced with amusement over the comedy of life than they brooded over its
tragedy. Although Edith was quick to appreciate Miss
Inglis's qualities as a "born" Matron (and a London-trained one, at that) until the end of their partnership, the
veil of reserve remained drawn between them.

40

In Shoreditch, Edith continued her practice of visiting newly discharged patients in their own homes — and now she went further. She began pestering committees administering convalescent homes in the country, or by the sea, for places for her saddest charges, offering at times to pay out of her own pocket when funds were low. Sometimes the children she sent away returned a little stronger . . . only to fade again as the damp and foul-smelling air of Shoreditch closed round them once more.

Edith was not discouraged. She hardly ever hoped for a complete recovery; but at least the children she managed to send away had one bright memory of sunshine and flowers, trees and sky, and sunlight on the water to carry back with them into the darkness of the slums. It was not much, perhaps, but it was something.

Her nursing experience was opening out in other ways, too. She had begun to lecture to the senior probationers, and here she found her skill at drawing invaluable. The delicate water colors of the English countryside now gave way to anatomical diagrams, but the basic skill she needed and possessed were the same.

Teaching was overtaking learning by now and it became overwhelmingly clear that this was where her true vocation lay. To save one sick child was a work of mercy, but to hand on her training to twenty new nurses might mean the gift of life and happiness to twenty sick children. Never in the slightest degree conceited, she knew her own worth both as a nurse and a teacher, and the years at Shoreditch merely served to convince her that it was in the latter field that her best work would be done.

But she had been nursing for ten long years; nursing in conditions of appalling difficulty, even though the lot of nurses was yearly growing more bearable. She was forty years old and feeling the strain — conscious too that she had reached a turning point in her career, but unable as yet to see the road ahead clearly.

Then, in 1906 came an opportunity to stand aside and see her life and work in perspective. As usual, it was to Miss Lückes that she turned with her problem. On January 12th she wrote:

> . . . The chance [of a break] has just come to me through the proposal of a friend that I should accompany her to the south of England, and possibly abroad, for three months from April or May. I am very anxious to accept, but fear it would be difficult to find another suitable post. I have now been here over two years and feel I have learned all there is to learn in one branch under the Poor Law. Would you very kindly help me in August — when I should be ready to return to work — if I wrote to you then? . . .

Miss Lückes reply to this frank and characteristic letter has been lost, but scribbled across it in now-faded pencil are the comforting words: "Yes, will certainly help her get fresh work." And it was with this knowledge to set her mind at rest that Edith turned her back on the squalor of Shoreditch and set out for the blue lakes and white-capped mountains of Europe.

The friend mentioned in her letter to Miss Lückes was Evaline Dickenson, with whom Edith had trained and worked at the London, and whose steadfast companion-ship had been the one close relationship she had formed outside her family.

This long holiday was the first, and last, time they were ever to know real leisure together, for when the months of carefree traveling were over Evaline was to marry and move to Ireland. Thus the one deep friendship of Edith's life was drawing to its close. In the future only a tenuous ribbon of letters was to hold them together.

After the vacation, finding a post equal to the one she had left proved an even greater problem than she had expected. In the ten years of her apprenticeship and growing authority in her profession, its popularity had spread among the women of England seeking either independence or a life of service. There were still very few occupations open to women in which they could regard themselves as professionally qualified, and though nursing still had many unpleasantnesses, its prestige had risen enormously. It had, in fact, become a fashionable occupation.

Several weeks after her return from her vacation with Evaline she was still looking for the elusive job which she felt must be waiting for her somewhere. In desperation she wrote to Miss Lückes again:

> . . . I have been trying for some time to obtain a post of trust — as Matron or Superintendent in an Institution, but so far without success. The posts with a fair salary are so much sought after and I cannot afford to take less than £60 or £70 . . . I have very good testimonials from Miss Inglis and the Medical Superintendent and I will enclose a

copy of the latter for you to see. I am greatly bene-
fitted in every way by my long and pleasant holiday
and feel quite ready to begin work again in earnest . . .

If Edith ever in her life felt impatient it must have been
at this time. Since the moment of her decision to make
nursing her life work, progress had been steady and satisfying. Why, she must have wondered, this pause — this
frustration? She had so much to offer, so much she longed
to pass on to the eager new generation pouring into the
hospitals and infirmaries. Things she had learned not only
with her ears and eyes and hands, but through the very
pores of her skin and the ends of her nerves, from the
skillful teachers of her old hospital.

"I still keep my old lectures on [sick room cookery] and
other subjects . . ." she continued sadly in her letter to
Miss Lückes, "and have found them useful over and over
again . . ."

A small fear clutched at her heart as she stuck down the
flap of the envelope. Would she find them so useful in
the future? But surely her work was not over yet? Surely
somewhere there was a job waiting to be done which only
she could usefully do?

When the job eventually did turn up, after weeks of
anxious waiting and searching, it was not at all in the
form Edith expected. The sister of a friend wrote to ask
whether she would consider working for a short time as a
Queen's District Nurse in the north of England. Edith
hesitated. This was quite unlike any work she had done

44

before; something for which she had not been trained, nor was it what she would have chosen. But it was work, and quite apart from the fact that she was anxious to be in harness once more, she needed the money. She had no private income and there was always, at the back of her mind, the thought that her parents were aging and might one day become at least partly dependent on her. And this job might, after all, be a way of learning more about her profession.

The Queen Victoria Jubilee District Nursing movement had been started in Liverpool in 1859, and by 1863 it had spread to Manchester. By the time Edith accepted her temporary post in 1906 it was well established.

Nursing in this way was quite different from anything she had done before, apart from the very brief period of emergency work in Maidstone during the typhoid epidemic. There was no hospital; the nurses lived together in a square, brick-built, gloomy house in one of the poor quarters of Manchester, cut off from the road by a high, prison-like wall. Inside the house was dark and dingy, and the only view from the windows was the winding gear of a coal mine.

From this barracklike building the nurses went out daily to visit their patients in their own homes, as they do to this day. Coming from the milder climate of the south, Edith at first felt that she had come to a country more foreign in some ways than even Belgium had been. Low gray clouds seemed to hang permanently over the soot-speckled buildings, and the wind carried a bleak dampness which crept

45

under the blue cloak of her uniform and chilled her bones:
even more thoroughly than the dry, bracing winds of a
Norfolk winter had done.

Time slipped by. Weeks became months. The high-
walled house in Ashton New Road became "home." Once
again it looked as if the backwaters had claimed her; that
life was standing still. And then something happened
which was later to make Edith see her time in Manchester
as an important part of the pattern of her life, though at
the time she did not see how vital it was. Again she wrote
to Miss Lückes, in a letter dated March 12th, 1907.

> You know, I believe, that I obtained a temporary
> post in Manchester at one of the Queen's District
> Homes, and that I have been acting as a nurse
> there. I have remained since September last,
> though the engagement was only originally for six
> weeks.
>
> Lately the Matron — sister of Miss Hall of the
> Seaman's Hospital — became very seriously ill and
> on Saturday underwent a severe operation which
> will prevent her from being on duty for several
> months. The Matronship is in my hands for the
> time being — the Committee having asked me to
> take charge. I feel it rather a heavy responsibility
> as I know so very little of the "Queen's" work or
> the etiquette of this branch of the work, but I feel
> I must try to fill the gap to the best of my abil-
> ity . . .
>
> It has been a terribly anxious time as there was
> the nursing of Miss Hall as well as the charge of
> the Home, which involves much bookkeeping . . .

It was an anxious time, and an arduous one, but it was to be of tremendous value to Edith in the years that followed. For a while her authority was supreme in her little kingdom, but it was not, of course, to last long. Miss Hall, the official Matron, was struggling back to health, and with her return Edith's task would end. Beyond that point the future was once more blank, though she had little time during those busy months to worry about the next step. And she was content to leave the future in the hands of God, who had so often in the past answered her prayers and questions in His own way. She was sure now that when the time came for the next change, He would point the way once more.

6

DOWNSTAIRS a door slammed violently and the windows of the boudoir rattled. Madame Depage, wife of the most eminent surgeon in Brussels, looked up from her writing desk with an inward sigh. Oh dear, she thought, Antoine was angry again. That was the third time this week he had come home from the hospital in a temper. What could it be this time? Had the Reverend Mother Hélène been difficult again?

She blotted the letter on her desk carefully and pushed back her chair, but before she could stand up the door burst open and her husband irrupted into the room. His face was scarlet with annoyance, his eyes flashing all-too-familiar danger signals.

"That *fool* of a woman!" he exploded.

"Antoine — please . . . the servants!" Madame Depage cast a nervous glance at the still half-open door. It was already obvious to her that the Reverend Mother Hélène had indeed been "difficult" again, but one did not refer in such terms to the august head of a religious order, however irritating; at least within hearing of the domestic staff. Quickly she crossed the room and closed the door.

"What is it this time?"

Dr. Depage flung himself into a chair by the window and drummed his fingers moodily on the small table by his side.

"You know how long I have spent training Sister Catherine in the work of the operating theater?" His wife nodded. Dissatisfied though her perfectionist husband often was with the work of the nuns who staffed his hospital, occasionally he found one who pleased him, and when this happened he spared no pains in training her in his ways. Sister Catherine had been just such a nurse, and her skill and devotion to the patients had made not only the running of the hospital, but the Depages' domestic life smoother and happier during the past few months.

"Don't tell me that Mother Hélène . . ." she began apprehensively.

The doctor bounced out of his chair and stormed up and down the room. "Ordered her back to the convent this morning . . ." he shouted, his face almost purple with fury. "Knowing full well that I had eight patients waiting for operations." His fist crashed down on the mantelpiece, setting the fragile ornaments dancing and jingling, but his wife hardly noticed the danger to her treasures in her concern.

"But surely . . ." she began.

". . . there's something I can do to stop it?" The doctor laughed bitterly. "You should know better than that by now, Marie. Why, even the Archbishop can't stop her. In her own convent she's a . . . a sort of goddess. And you know what pleasure it gives her to annoy me."

"Perhaps, my dear, you are not always very tactful," his wife reminded him mildly. "More than once I've heard you grumbling that the nurses are not as clean as they might be . . ."

"How can they be clean, wearing those filthy black robes . . . utterly unsuitable in a hospital." Dr. Depage grumbled.

"But it is the rule of their Order."

"Maybe. But a hospital isn't a convent."

Madame Depage sighed. This was an argument she had heard so often before, and to which there seemed no adequate reply. As long as the convents provided the nurses the Belgian hospitals needed so desperately, the battle would go on. And if the convents withdrew the supply of nurses — which might easily happen if her husband continued his autocratic ways — who was to take their place?

"Something will have to be done, Marie." The doctor spoke more quietly, though there was a note of desperation in his voice. The choleric color had drained from his face and he slumped down again into his chair. "Things can't go on like this."

"But what can you do?" Madame Depage moved over to him and smoothed back the tousled hair from his forehead. His face was unnaturally pale now, and she was anxiously aware of the lines of strain round his mouth, the shadows under his eyes.

He shook his head wearily. "Heaven alone knows. But

50

we can't go on being at the mercy of the whims of people like the Reverend Mother Hélène, who can snatch away nurses to staff the convent hospitals the moment I've finished training them." He jumped restlessly to his feet again and paced up and down. "We must have more lay nurses — women who are not under the domination of the church."

"But Antoine, you know that doesn't work. No decent, well-educated girl will take on the job — and the others are worse than useless. If you turn the nuns out of the hospitals, you will have no nurses at all."

"It works in England," Dr. Depage retorted stubbornly.

His wife smiled a little sadly. "Yes — in England. But Belgium, alas, has no Miss Nightingale to lead and inspire her young women."

"Then we must find a Miss Nightingale." Dr. Depage swung round and caught his wife's arm, shaking her gently with a return of his more familiar exuberance. "We will find a Miss Nightingale, my love."

In spite of herself, Marie Depage laughed at the sudden change in her husband's mood, from despair to optimism. "And where will you find another Miss Nightingale, Antoine?" she teased him gently.

"Where but in England — the country which bred Miss Nightingale herself?" Dr. Depage paused in his restless prowling as if, having spoken without thought, he had spontaneously answered the question that was in his own mind, too. "Yes, of course Marie," he went on excitedly. "In England there must be hundreds, perhaps thousands, of first-class, well-trained nurses by now. Among them all

51

surely there must be one with enough skill and knowledge — and enough love for her work — to help us found a Belgian nursing service?"

There was a long moment's silence while they looked at one another and the seed of the idea took root in their minds, grew and blossomed.

"She would need more than skill and knowledge, Antoine," Marie Depage said slowly, at last. "She would need a great deal of courage and endurance, too. You know how jealous the Church is of its power. It will not give up its rights in the hospitals without a struggle. And how can you be sure that Belgian women will follow the example of a foreigner? We have always resented outside interference in our affairs. In England it was different — Miss Nightingale was among her own people."

"Enough, Marie. You make difficulties," the doctor interrupted impatiently. "Too many exist already. We must be more constructive. First . . ." He held up a hand and ticked off the points on his outspread fingers. ". . . first we must have the support of the medical profession. That should not be difficult — the other doctors are just as tired as I am of the whims and fancies of the Reverend Mother. Secondly, we must change the attitude of our young women to the idea of nursing. We must make it 'respectable' . . . even a little exciting, if such a thing is possible," he added with a grimace.

Madame Depage laughed. "That will, I think, appeal to them more," she agreed ruefully, "though it might be useful to persuade their *mothers* that nursing is a respectable occupation."

The doctor snapped his fingers. "An inspiration, my dear . . . ! A Committee of Ladies from fashionable society is just what we need to launch the scheme. Let *them* persuade our mothers that they approve of nursing."

"And how do you persuade these ladies, in the first place?" Marie inquired, smiling indulgently, relieved at the return of her husband's good spirits, but only half persuaded of the practicability of his idea.

"I've already told you." The doctor chuckled mischievously. "Form them into a Committee. Have you ever met a woman who could resist an invitation to sit on a Committee? And once having accepted the invitation, would do anything but believe wholeheartedly in its objects?" Still chuckling he sat down at her desk, pushed aside the letter she had been writing, and picked up her pen. "Now who, among your friends, can we persuade to help us, my dear?"

Part
II

7

IT WAS a damp, depressing day in spring when the letter arrived on Edith's desk. She eyed it curiously. She was not expecting a letter from Brussels, and the writing was unfamiliar. Could it be news of the François family? If so, coming from a stranger it must be bad news! She slit the envelope quickly and glanced at the signature. "Depage": the name meant nothing to her; but the letter was a long one. She settled down to read.

After she had finished reading she sat very still for a long time, oblivious of the beating of the rain on the window. A jumble of emotions swayed her this way and that as she turned the closely written pages once more: elation . . . gratitude . . . awe . . . uncertainty.

It was such a very *big* job she was being asked to do. A job ultimately involving the welfare of a whole nation; and it needed a "big" person to do it. Was she really that person? Why had she been chosen, out of the many thousands of nurses in England?

"Look back," a small voice inside her seemed to say.

"Look back over your life, and you will see the signposts leading to this moment."

She looked up at the window beside her desk. Little trickles of sooty rain smeared the glass, but she did not see them. She did not see the winding gear of the mine shaft which lay only a few hundred yards from where she was sitting, or the clouds, heavy with more rain, in the sky above it. She was seeing, instead, the panorama of her life.

Had she done so a few weeks before it would have seemed that it had no special direction. Now, holding Dr. Depage's letter in her hand and staring through the rain-streaked windows, it seemed one word was written large and clear at every turn and twist of life's road: "Belgium."

Summer was already beginning to slip downhill when she packed her trunks for the last, and most fateful, move of her life, but she saw nothing symbolic in the autumn and winter months stretching ahead. Her mood was more one of spring — a new beginning. On the long train journey down to the Channel coast she said a temporary goodbye to the well-loved countryside of England, but it was a goodbye without sadness. She would come home often for holidays, she promised herself. As soon as the Belgian School of Nursing was established and things were running smoothly. Of course that would not be for a little while yet, but it was not goodbye forever to the England she loved.

As the coastline of Belgium rose, flat and hazy, from the sea the last thoughts of home were put behind her and her mind stretched eagerly forward to what lay ahead.

It was twelve years since she had left that beloved country; twelve years so crowded with experiences, training and preparation that there had been little time for her to spend in dreaming of the people left behind in Brussels. But they had not forgotten her, as she now knew. Marguerite François had grown up, and was Marguerite François no longer. Her mother-in-law, Dr. Depage had written, was a member of the Ladies' Committee that was helping him with the arrangements for founding his new school of nursing in Brussels . . .

It was just one small piece of the pattern over which Edith had sat looking back in her little office in Manchester; but it was a tremendously important one. As she slipped it into its place she accepted, with quiet joy, the future which lay before her. And having accepted it, she set to work, in her usual practical manner, to plan the new venture.

Already Edith saw beyond the empty rooms of the ill-adapted terrace houses to the school as it might be in the future. She saw a big white hospital, shining with cleanliness, set in a beautiful garden; wards light and airy, painted in soft, bright colors; operating theaters equipped with every modern device; kitchens staffed by efficient cooks, trained in the art of hospital dietetics; neatly uniformed nurses, moving with quiet authority.

> I believe [she wrote to Miss Lückes], we shall begin with a few pupils — I have made a point of educated women as the first-trained nurses will become the teachers ultimately — and a few patients. This will I hope develop rapidly into a fair-sized training school, so that there may be plenty of ma-

terial for the work. Looking forward I hope that in time both Private and District nursing may spring from this beginning as the need for both is, I believe, greatly felt and people are no longer willing to put up with the old class of nurse. I am going over in August to get everything in readiness . . .

Edith knew, of course, that there must be a hundred details waiting for her to settle immediately on arrival. She even hoped, a little guiltily, that she would be left to settle most of them on her own. Committees of Ladies, it was well known, were apt to want a finger in every pie, even technical ones about which they had no useful knowledge — and even more apt to sulk if they were, however tactfully, firmly excluded.

On this point she need not have worried unduly. August and September were traditionally holiday months for Belgian society, and it had not occurred to any of the Committee Ladies to allow such a mundane occasion as the starting of a national nursing service to interfere with their social engagements.

I arrived two days ago [Edith wrote ruefully to Miss Lückes on September 19], and found the four houses which have been made to communicate only partly furnished and in much confusion, and the Committee absent on holiday except the Secretary and the President who returned for a day or two to welcome me . . . no servants; only a portress, and nothing finished but my sitting-room — and we have to open on October 1st!

60

The few Committee members who were available during those first hectic days proved at best broken reeds, and at worst stumbling blocks to some of her most treasured plans.

". . . the Committee think night nurses are not necessary — that if a nurse sleeps on the same floor with the patients, that is sufficient," she went on dejectedly, and in a burst of mild exasperation she added: "Just now there is no-one to refer to and no money, and many necessities wanting. Everyone is very keen, and very indefinite. They make notes on paper of things needed, and there it ends . . ."

How often, during those very early days, even the inexhaustible patience of Edith Cavell must have been tried by her willing, but inefficient Ladies. But if the Ladies' Committee were less than efficient, the doctors had at least made an effort to plan out the nurses' training in a way which met with her full approval, and her letter continues on a much more cheerful note.

> The nurses sign on for five years — three for training and two to be passed in private or institution nursing, in the service of the school. At the end of that time they will receive their diploma and be able to leave. There are to be numerous lectures and in the second year the nurses will go to the Surgical Institute opposite for their surgical training . . .

It is here, having skillfully worked up to the point, that Edith reached the real reason for her letter: a request

61

which was to be duplicated over and over again during the year which followed.

For this Institute, which belongs to the first Surgeon in Belgium, M. Depage, a Matron is wanted and he wished me to write and ask you if you could send him one. It is a fine, new building with two beautiful theatres and eleven rooms for patients — tho' roughly adapted and designed by him to fit the needs of modern surgery. He wants a nurse who will be able to arrange all his operations and be present to assist him — who will act as his matron, train the nurses and keep certain books.

He will give her £50 a year and I think it will be an excellent post. She must speak French fairly well of course. Also he wants three trained nurses to work under her — he offers only £24 for the first year and they need not have very much knowledge of French.

The Institute opens in November. Perhaps from the point of view of money it does not seem worth having, but I do think it is work that greatly needs doing and that those who come out should do so with the object of helping on this new movement which if started on the right lines should be of the greatest possible benefit to this country. It is pioneer work here and needs much enthusiasm and courage and intelligence and as there are many still looking askance at it, it will require great tact also. M. Depage desires that there should exist a cordial feeling and intercourse between these two Institutions and that I should be regarded as the

Head Matron, and that other branches should be opened in course of time to which my probationers should go to learn fever work, midwifery etc. Thus we might eventually have a colony of English women here as heads of the branches, if we who come first can make a success of it . . .

Here was a dream, and an aim, indeed! A dream that was opening out, its scope broadening. Edith could see a great drawing-together of her two countries: that of her birth and that of her adoption; the one bringing to the other the knowledge, skill and dedicated unselfishness it so badly needed. It was a dream she kept always before her, and one which gave her the extra patience and forbearance she needed to face the delays, the frustrations and the problems.

For as the dream expanded, so did the difficulties. As she said in her letter, there were many who looked on the new venture with disfavor. By the well-born and well-educated Belgian woman, nursing was still regarded, as in England it had been regarded in the pre-Florence Nightingale era, as "low-class" work, beneath their dignity; something to be left where it had always been, in the hands of the nuns. And the Church authorities, as Madame Depage had foreseen, were in their turn only too anxious to retain their rights; quick to point out that the head of the new Nursing Service was not only a foreigner, but a non-Catholic in a Catholic country.

Instead of being greeted as a benefactor, Edith found herself treated, beyond the small circle of enthusiasts, with suspicion and resentment. Only four probationers applied for training at the opening of the school, and the modest blue and white uniform she designed for them was met with jeers by outsiders as "fancy dress." Workmen, meeting the probationers in the rue de la Culture, called ribald remarks after them, and even threw stones.

"This isn't carnival time," they mocked.

The girls themselves, brought up in the free-and-easy atmosphere of Brussels, did not understand the meaning of self-discipline. They arrived late on duty, chattered and gossiped when they should have been working, and flatly refused to accept the month of night duty which was a part of their contract. They would, they declared, do no more than a week at any one time.

Edith, shocked and dismayed by this lack of seriousness towards what to her was a life of utter devotion, fought down her instinct for strictness. Tact, as she had told Miss Lückes in her first report, was one of the first essentials in the work she was doing, and it never deserted her. Though she knew in her heart that a month of night duty by all the nurses was essential to the smooth running of the Clinic, she also knew that to insist on it might mean the resignation of her first four precious probationers — and that if they left in a disgruntled mood the news would soon spread, and no more Belgian nurses would be forthcoming.

With dignity and almost superhuman restraint, she refrained from enforcing what she knew to be right, not only in the interests of the hospital, but of the girls themselves, and a few weeks later she had her reward.

". . . the probationers are making more progress," she wrote to Miss Lückes only a month after the rebellion. "I think they are beginning to regret their short night duty, but I am not appearing to know that at present."

She had not much longer to wait. Only a very few weeks were needed to persuade the probationers that seven days on "nights" resulted in their being sleepy on duty and sleepless when they were off. It needed at least a month to establish themselves in the new routine.

It was a triumph for patience and understanding, but if she felt triumphant, Edith did not show it. She knew only too well that, new as they were both to the idea of nursing and nursing itself, the Belgian girls would have to learn much by experience that she had learned by obedience to discipline.

And she remembered, when they were most trying, that a Belgian girl still needed courage to become a nurse at all. Disapproved of by their parents and friends, jeered at by people in the street — looked down on, in the early stages, even by the servants, the first probationers had almost as much as their Matron to contend with. Small wonder that occasionally they rebelled against the unaccustomed strait-jacket of disciplined training.

8

Two PEOPLE who believed as passionately in what they were doing as Edith Cavell and Antoine Depage might have been expected to work in harmony, but the truth is that from the beginning their wills and their ways clashed like resounding brass cymbals.

Temperamentally they were as far apart as fire and water. Dr. Depage was the child of poor parents, just as Edith was, but there the resemblance ceased. Dr. Depage had not lived his early life in a sheltered backwater; he had fought every inch of the way up the ladder to brilliant success, and had never had time to acquire a polished veneer. The Reverend Mother Hélène was not the only person to provoke him, and when roused he had a tongue as blunt as a hammer and a temper as uncertain as the English weather Edith had left behind her.

She was horrified and offended by his violent language when something displeased him, which it often did in the early days. She never openly quarreled with him, but her obstinacy in matters over which they disagreed was just as great as his; whereas he would rage and shout and swear, she would sit in icy silence, or speak with a quiet firmness which he found equally infuriating.

More than once the wonderful new nursing service came near to being wrecked on the twin rocks of Dr. Depage's irascibility and Nurse Cavell's puritanical reserve, and it might have done so if it had not been for Marie Depage's saving grace of humor — a quality which both her husband and Edith lacked — and the tact to hide the twinkle in her eyes which danced whenever the two irreconcilable forces met.

Quite early in the school's existence one of the young probationers, still unused to the minor details of hospital etiquette, offended the great doctor's idea of what was proper.

She could hardly have chosen a worse morning. Dr. Depage had spent the previous day operating in difficult circumstances, on a difficult case. He had been visiting patients until late in the evening, and a number of problems in connection with the new training school had cropped up after that. He was tired and harassed; impatient with the slowness with which the new venture was getting under way and inclined to be critical of everything in the new nursing home from the patients' diet to the color of the paint. The young nurse's carelessness was the last straw.

In a towering rage he burst into the office where Matron Cavell was sitting at work on the interminable accounts of the School, his face purple as a ripe plum with temper. A torrent of abusive language poured from his lips so fast that for some time she was unable to disentangle the cause of the uproar, but at last she gleaned the fact that he was annoyed with one of the nurses.

Carefully she put the pen she was holding on the desk. Irritating though she knew the nurses could be, they were her "children," and she was prepared to defend any one of them against the overbearing doctor, provided her crime had not been too heinous.

"But what did the nurse do, Doctor?" she asked quietly, when there was a momentary pause in the tirade.

"Did I not tell you?" Dr. Depage strode to the window and hammered on the sill with his clenched fist. "She was improperly dressed on duty. She must go — at once."

Improperly dressed! Edith caught her breath. What had the nurses been up to now?

"In what way was she — improperly dressed, Dr. Depage?" she asked.

"Her collar — I told you — it was not a stiff one. It was without starch," he roared impatiently.

"I see." Edith could scarcely keep the note of relief out of her voice. "But surely that is hardly sufficient reason for dismissal? You know how short of nurses we are, Doctor . . . and after all, these young girls are not yet used to the idea of uniform."

Her mild explanation was cut short by another torrent of anger. "It's time these so-and-so nurses learned some something-or-other discipline . . ." Dr. Depage barked — among other things.

Quietly Nurse Cavell rose to her feet and crossed to the door. "I am afraid I cannot discuss the matter further with you while you continue to use such objectionable language,

Dr. Depage," she said firmly, her eyes — usually so full of sympathy — as cold as the flints of Swardeston Church. "Perhaps we can take up the matter when you are more yourself."

She shut the door of the office noiselessly behind her, leaving Dr. Depage open-mouthed and, for once, silenced.

They did not meet again that day, and goodness only knows what would have happened when they next met if Madame Depage had not suspected that something had gone wrong between them and wheedled most of the story out of her grumpy husband later in the day. With a sigh and a smile she put on her hat, called a cab, and drove round to the School in the rue de la Culture.

Nurse Cavell welcomed her pleasantly; she was already growing fond of the charming wife of her difficult colleague, and it was not long before Marie was hearing the other side of the story — which she had already half guessed.

"I do understand that my husband is a little — trying at times," she agreed sympathetically. "But he means no harm. It is just his way. I hope you will forgive him. He works so hard and has the school so much at heart; but sometimes his tongue runs away with him. Just now he is not sleeping very well. Perhaps if you could arrange the nurse's duties so that for a little while they do not meet, he will forget what has happened. I hope that perhaps you can forget, too?"

It was the first, but by no means the last time that she was to pour oil on the troubled waters, and her patient understanding of two widely differing natures was to maintain an uneasy peace at the rue de la Culture school.

Meanwhile, there were other small disappointments, other small triumphs to fill the busy days that flew quickly past. In spite of Marie Depage's friendship, Edith still felt herself very alone with her problems and it was, as always, to Miss Lückes she turned not only for help, but for an outlet for her worries. Writing to her old Matron helped to clarify her thoughts and bolster up her sometimes flagging optimism:

> M. Depage has now decided to take three Dutch nurses trained, or partly trained, in Holland as they do not expect so much salary [she wrote regretfully about a month after her arrival in Brussels]. I am sorry he did not wait to see if English women would have been found to come out, but as they will have nothing to do with the training of the probationers, it will not make so much difference.

The first bright dream of an all-English staff was beginning to fade. But she was determined not to be downhearted.

> We are quite cosmopolitan here, and speak among us many languages [she went on cheerfully]. Two of my pupils seem likely to make excellent nurses; they are very devoted to the patients and the work. I find them unpunctual and rather noisy, but the patients are devoted to them also, and we already have a reputation for nursing well! We have four patients at present and others coming. I anticipate having the beds always full, but

unfortunately women are not offering well for the work. I have only four at present, one of whom is off duty and does not seem likely to be very suitable. I have written an article which I hope will be published shortly, and which we hope may induce some to join.

The lectures begin this week . . .

One step forward, and two steps back . . . two steps forward and one step back. Sometimes it seemed that she was getting no further. Sometimes that she never would get any further. But opposition only strengthened her determination. Pinpricks and open attacks alike failed to move her from her purpose.

Each night when she put her head on the pillow of her narrow bed it seemed a miracle that the school was still in existence; and each new day she opened her eyes to a long list of questions, objections and restrictions.

How best, without offending them, explain to the doctors that certain duties, such as bedmaking, belonged not to them, but the nurses? How to persuade the patients that it was unnecessary to *bribe* the nurses to wash them? How discourage the patients' friends from smuggling in extra food, and invading the kitchen premises to cook it? No one, except herself, seemed to have the faintest idea of how a hospital should be run. Every tiny detail of the work, down to the dusting of the wards, had to be supervised, in addition to the arrangement of classes and instruction of the raw new nurses in their technical work.

The soft brown hair Edith had inherited from her mother soon began to show streaks of gray. She seemed

71

to grow smaller, and slighter, as the months passed; but the flame that burned within her burned steadily. Nothing was too much trouble; no detail too small for her attention, and nothing missed the serene gray eyes on her daily round of the wards and patients' rooms.

Always before her she had the ideal of her own training, and she knew that as the new nursing service in Belgium began, so it would continue. The standards set by the first probationers would be those they passed on to the long line of those who were to come later; and it was by their behavior that the great jury of the Belgian people would judge the success or failure of her work.

It was an uphill struggle, but gradually — very gradually — the young nurses began to understand that those standards were her personal ones too. Like the François children they grew to realize that, strict though Nurse Cavell was, she never expected more of them than she did of herself. Though she might at times seem severe, there was always good sense and good reason for the rules and regulations that seemed to hem them in on every side.

She had a genius for teaching lessons which stuck in their minds. Walking past a patient's room one morning, her ear was caught by a scuffling noise inside. Opening the door she found one of the youngest probationers, broom in hand, chasing up and down. The girl stopped awkwardly at the sight of Matron's disapproving face.

"It's a spider, Madame," she burst out defensively. "A huge one. I was only trying to kill it."

If she expected commendation she was doomed to disappointment. Gently Nurse Cavell took the broom from her hand.

"Don't do that, nurse," she said quietly. "Catch the spider, and put it outside." She paused. "And remember, always, that to a nurse even the lowest form of life is sacred. It is our duty to preserve, never to destroy."

Thoughtfully the little nurse watched the door close behind the retreating back. It was a tiny incident, over in a few seconds, but it taught her one of the greatest lessons of her professional life — one which she never forgot.

9

FOR THE first three months Edith felt that she was walking along a tightrope over a bottomless pit. If she leaned too far to one side she risked offending someone who could wreck the precious school; if she leaned too far to the other, she would be false to her own ideals — something equally unthinkable.

Something was needed to draw all of those concerned in the new venture closer in understanding — something about which they all felt deeply, and which they all understood in the same way. When it came it was something outside nursing altogether, yet which touches every hospital, and everyone who works in one with a special magic: Christmas!

Sitting alone in her small sitting room as the December nights closed in, Edith remembered wistfully the Christmases she had spent at the London — the holly and tinsel, the carols; the flushed, smiling faces of the patients; the special meals; the little entertainments in the wards and the moving services on Christmas morning. She could not remember a Hospital Christmas which had not left her with a sense of exaltation, and a heightened feeling of affection for the hospital and everyone in it. Perhaps . . . was it possible that a miracle would occur in the rue de la Culture too, this Christmas?

For once she was not disappointed. When the first gray light of Christmas Day groped its way into the nurses' dining room it touched the soft green-and-silver-decorated branches of a little tree — the gift of the sometimes-fault-finding Ladies' Committee. Later in the day the nurses gathered round it, twittering with delight over the packages which mingled with the decorations. A small ceremony marked the handing out of gifts, the gracious Ladies of the Committee fully enjoying their role of Father Christmas. There was, perhaps, the faintest twinkle in the eye of the one who handed Edith a kettle on a stand — precious tea-making apparatus: an olive branch of reconciliation over one of their minor skirmishes! Edith accepted it with grave pleasure, missing the twinkle, but accepting the tacit apology with dignity.

In the evening there was a party for both nurses and patients, and when the lights finally winked out along the rows of windows, leaving only the dim night lights of the wards to burn steadily through the long hours of darkness, heads rested more contentedly on the pillows of the narrow beds than they had done since the first turbulent days of the school's opening.

Lying alone in her austere room, Edith sent up a prayer of thankfulness for the drawing together of nurses, patients and patrons under the influence of the Christmas spirit. It was, she knew, only a truce — a temporary lull in the stormy growth of the school, but surely nothing could ever be quite the same again. Christmas had turned them into a family, and in the future their quarrels would be family quarrels.

Within a few days the aromatic scent of the tree had faded; the floor of the dining room was littered with pine needles and the silver decorations were dull and tarnished. Outside, the street was swept by blustery rain and inside the problems began to pile up again. There *was* a greater feeling of comradeship, but the battle was far from over.

Miss Maude, a trained nurse sent out as a result of an S O S, to Miss Lückes, to act as Matron at Dr. Depage's Surgical Institute, had proved to be a disappointment, both to Nurse Cavell and the explosive doctor. Her French was almost nonexistent. She was completely bewildered by the ways of her new colleagues and patients, and showed very little promise of adapting herself to them. Puzzled by the strangeness of the new country, and often hurt by M. Depage's lack of tolerance, her small stock of self-confidence dwindled; and as it grew less, the doctor's exasperation, and the tension between them, grew to a point where even Nurse Cavell had reluctantly to agree that the experiment was a failure.

It was distressing not only for Edith, but for Miss Maude herself, who had come from England with high hopes of her new appointment, to find herself relegated to the position of Chief Nurse under a Matron whose knowledge of French made her more able to handle the housekeeping and reception of patients. But she accepted the position with good grace, and Edith's disappointment was soon

76

swamped in a flood of other problems, not the least being the gradual realization that Miss Maude was far from being the only English nurse to prove a disappointment. Too often those who offered themselves for the new Belgian nursing service looked on it not so much as an opportunity to spread enlightenment as an escape from Victorian England into the freer life of the Continent; so that their influence over the giddy young Belgian girls was far from what their Matron had hoped.

In front of her colleagues and her patients she hid her disappointment. Only occasionally did a note of bitterness creep into her letters to Miss Lückes. During a brief holiday in England she wrote:

> I greatly valued your letter. The help and encouragement you have given me come at a time when I much needed it, for the difficulties are many — especially with the pupils, and even since I have been away there has been some wrong-doing and disloyalty among them . . .

It seemed that she could not relax her vigilence, even for a moment, for the standards she set to slip backward. She might have been forgiven if she had given up the struggle; had turned her back angrily on the people she was trying so hard to serve, and left them to fight on alone, a losing battle. But that was not her way, and in spite of their childish resentment and slowness to appreciate her work, she loved the Belgian people.

By the early spring of 1908 things were beginning to run a little more smoothly. There were still plenty of problems, but a pattern was beginning to emerge from the chaos she had found the previous autumn on her arrival in Brussels. By April she felt satisfied enough with the progress she had made to send a report back to the English *Nursing Mirror.* In it she said:

> The first house, employed as the nurses' home, was opened last October. It is comfortably fitted up; it has bedrooms for about twelve nurses, a sitting-room and a large dining-room with a piano, as well as the matron's office. The three adjoining houses contain twenty-four bedrooms for patients, who pay from five to eight francs a day, a lecture room, consulting and waiting rooms. Each nurse will have a floor containing three or four patients to look after, but a special nurse will be put on for bad cases, and there will be one night nurse to each house.
>
> In the bathroom are placed gas rings, that the nurses may boil water or instruments, and a small cupboard in which they may keep all necessaries for the purpose . . .
>
> The nurses breakfast at 7 o'clock, wash their patients and give them their meals at eight. The house doctor comes at 8.30 and all the pupils accompany him on his round and carry out his orders when he leaves. The bathrooms are then tidied and the nurses dress, do their own rooms and have lunch. At twelve o'clock dinner is served to the patients and at 12.30 to the nurses. As the early breakfast consists of coffee and bread and butter only, according to national custom, they are ready

78

to do full justice to the soup, meat and dessert provided. At four o'clock they have tea, after the English fashion recently adopted here, the patients being served first. Beds are made, treatments carried out, and everything settled for the night when supper is carried up at 7 P.M. The nurses have their own supper at 7.30. It generally consists of meat, vegetables and cheese. Every nurse has two hours off duty each day, a half-day a week, which is extended once a month to a whole day and one month's holiday during the year.

There is a lecture given (in French) every weekday. The professors are well-known men and their classes most interesting and suitable. The following subjects are taken the first year: anatomy and physiology, hygiene, medical diseases, elementary pharmacology, care of the sick and sick nursing.

The probationers, who to be eligible must be between the ages of twenty and thirty-five, are provided with indoor uniform — outdoor uniform is not worn — and are given 180f. (£7.7.—) the first year, 240f. (£9.10.—) the second and 300f. (£12) the third year. Afterwards, payment is according to the work done for the school. Probationers, who may be of any nationality, upon acceptance sign for five years, after a two months' trial. Three years are devoted to training, the first in medical school, the second in gaining surgical experience; and the third learning to nurse infectious cases etc. In the fourth and fifth years the nurses will be employed in private work, hospitals or doctors' nursing homes as may be required . . .

79

The probationers wear blue cotton dresses with high white aprons, white linen sleeves to cover the forearm, which is bare beneath, Sister Dora caps without strings, and white collars. The contrast they present to the nuns in their heavy stuff robes, and the lay nurses in their grimy apparel is the contrast of the unhygienic past with the enlightened present. . . .

The greatest problem, for a time, remained the one of obtaining good, reliable, French-speaking nurses from England to carry out the training of the Belgian probationers. Poor Miss Lückes was subjected to a shower of requests for Sisters and trained nurses throughout 1908, and never seems to have lost patience, or willingness to help.

"I am so very grateful to you for sending me another Sister," Edith wrote during the summer. "It is a great anxiety to have women to train the nurses of whose work one is not sure, and whose loyalty is not certain . . ."

And again, a few weeks later:

Again I am in difficulties for a Sister. I engaged one, but she is not a good nurse and still less a good teacher. I am afraid I shall never be satisfied with any other than a Londoner to train the probationers. Other methods do not please me and I am anxious to introduce the very best into Belgium . . .

Her efforts, and her determination to have nothing but the best for her beloved School were to have their reward. News began to spread of the excellence of the nursing, and the training, to be obtained at the Berkendael Institute, as the school was sometimes called, and by the time the first anniversary of its founding came round she was able to write more optimistically:

> My new pupils are beginning to work. There will be seven at present to start the New Year, and I hope to have more before long. The four of the first year are now at the Surgical Institute under Miss Maude's care, where I think and hope they will do well and begin to prove useful. The lectures begin about the middle of this month and will consist of the same as were given last year with some on surgical nursing in addition . . .

A note almost of lighthearted mischief appeared then for the first time in this very one-track-minded correspondence. One can almost hear Edith chuckle as she went on: "One pupil arrived last night. I was out; it appears that her courage failed her on the doorstep and she ran back to her friends. I am hoping she will feel a little braver to-day and return."

It is not difficult to picture the new little nurse standing, with fluttering heart, one finger poised in front of the doorbell. Which of the stories she had heard about Nurse Cavell and her school were true? Was she really an angel in a dark blue dress — or an ogre, wickedly disguised to trap unwary young girls?

Alas, Edith leaves the story tantalizingly unfinished. We shall never know whether the little nurse gained fresh courage and learned the truth . . . whether she ever became one of those who, in Edith's own words, were "making a new profession for women"; who were "helping forward the cause of science . . . providing the best possible help for the sick and suffering."

10

IT HAD BEEN difficult enough for Edith to find, and make, friends during her nursing career in England. Evaline Dickenson was the only one who had managed to find her way past the cloak of reserve and dedication during the years in London. But in Brussels it became next to impossible. To begin with, every waking hour was absorbed in thoughts of the new school, and added to that, to draw one of the Sisters or nurses closer to her in intimacy would have been to court a disaster of jealousy and resentment among the others.

Edith had to remain aloof, careful to treat every one of her subordinates with the same reticent kindness; and there were very few opportunities to become intimate with anyone outside the school. Even here she felt she must walk warily, for her every movement was, to some, suspect until the school was an established success. She did make one friend, Miss Carter, an Englishwoman working as a Domestic Science teacher in one of the Brussels Council Schools, and it was with her that she spent an occasional hour of leisure when, for a little while, the Institute was running smoothly enough for her to leave it briefly.

But if human friendships were denied her, Edith found no such difficulties where animals were concerned. A constant and shifting population of stray dogs turned up at the doors of the school, begging for food — and there was a strict (if unwritten) rule that none was to be turned away until it had been fed and groomed back to sleek contentment, usually by Edith's own hands. After she died a little notebook filled with sketches and notes was found among her papers, giving careful directions and hints for the comfort of pet dogs, which showed eloquently how much she had at heart the welfare of her pets, most of whom moved on as soon as their immediate wants had been satisfied.

One or two, however, lingered, and one in particular, Jack, stayed to become Edith's constant companion for the last years of her life. The nurses, Committee and townsfolk viewed Edith's devotion to him, and the rest of the motley and migratory collection of dogs which pattered up and down the steps of 149 rue de la Culture, with a mixture of amusement and exasperation. Those who admired and felt affection for her smiled, and shrugged, as Monsieur and Madame François had smiled and shrugged over her eccentricities many years before; but those who had reservations about her and her work frowned disapprovingly. Surely it was against the laws of hygiene, about which one heard so much, so often, from Miss Cavell's own lips, to keep an animal — and a *stray* animal at that — in a nursing home?

But, argued Edith's partisans, poor Jack was scrubbed and disinfected within an inch of his life, and his coat brushed and trimmed with as much regularity as any of the patients was washed and tidied. Besides, they added a little impishly, was it not rather pleasant to find the almost perfect Miss Cavell possessed one little human weakness?

The disapprovers were unconvinced, and Jack continued to live at the school on sufferance — but he did continue to live there, and to provide Edith with solace and companionship during the most difficult years she had ever known. In the evenings, when the patients were finally settled and an uneasy peace fell over the Institute, she would slip out into the cool of the dusky evening and walk, as she had walked in other places at other times, with the companionable pad-pad of Jack's feet beside her, his pink tongue lolling and his bright, trusting eyes fixed on her face. Here was someone who believed in her utterly; who never doubted her motives or actions. She returned from those walks with a lighter step and a lighter heart, soothed and strengthened to face whatever the next day might bring.

Some of the problems the next day brought had their pleasant side; proving to her that the gradual uphill struggle was leading to a broadening and strengthening of her position in the medical life of Belgium. Other hospitals were beginning to ask for nurses trained by her methods: a sure sign of success. Shortly after the first anniversary of the opening of her school she was asked to find a Matron for the hospital of St. Jean, where most of the work was still in the hands of the nuns. Lay nurses had already been introduced into this hospital, but no arrangements had been made for their training. It was a delicate situation, as she warned Miss Lückes when, inevitably, she asked her for help.

> The conditions are not ideal [she wrote frankly]. Conflicts with the nuns would certainly take place if anyone became Matron who had not sufficient tact. This is distinctly undesirable. At the same time a good deal of courage and firmness is necessary to extend the school and make it a success. I believe the pupils are not all that could be wished, in fact the whole thing has to be made, but it should be a very good and influential position one of these days.

Finding the right person for such an obstacle-strewn task was a formidable proposition, but between them she and Miss Lückes discovered Miss Evans — a London-trained, French-speaking nurse who seemed in every way ideal. She worked for a short time under Edith, and it was with confidence and relief that she was able to send her out to spread yet further the "English" system of nursing.

But every nurse sent out in this way meant one less on her staff at the rue de la Culture, and one more to be found who reached her high standards. That they should reach these high standards, and be completely reliable, became increasingly vital as her own work spread farther and farther, and she was obliged to spend more and more of her time away from her own Institute.

By 1912 she was, in addition to running the Institute and nursing home in the rue de la Culture, in charge of Dr. Depage's nursing home; a new hospital, St. Gilles, and a growing body of nurses on private cases. To spread the news of their work she had started a nursing magazine: *L'Infirmière,* and she sent periodical reports to the English *Nursing Mirror,* all of which took up a great deal of her time. School nurses had also been introduced, and supervision of them fell to her, as well as an interest in the various hospitals and nursing homes to which she had sent nurses from time to time.

Altogether it was a life which left very little time for active nursing. Administrative work piled up; there were lectures to be given, reports to committees compiled, and a keen eye to be kept on the general work of the Institute to make sure that the work of the nurses never became slipshod, for she was still intensely aware that it was here, in the four inconvenient, linked houses in the rue de la Culture, that the lamp must be kept burning most brightly.

She still needed, desperately, women who understood and appreciated what she was trying to do. Women she could trust to carry on when she was absent as they would when her eyes were upon them. Women inspired by the same complete conviction as she was that this work was the greatest, and most rewarding that life had to offer them. It was a lot to ask. There are few enough Edith Cavells in the world at any one time; to expect to find more than one of them in any one place at once was asking for a miracle.

Then something like a miracle happened during the summer of 1912. Because Miss Lückes, willing as she was, was quite unable to satisfy all her needs, Edith had begun to advertise for staff in the *Nursing Mirror.* She was on holiday with her mother — a luxury she allowed herself once a year, realizing no doubt that such a "luxury" was a necessity if she were not to drive herself to the verge of a physical and mental breakdown — when a letter came in answer to her latest appeal in the columns of the *Mirror.* It was signed Elisabeth Wilkins, and the address was a hospital in Cardiff, on the south coast of Wales. The writer claimed a thorough training in nursing, plus an excellent command of French, learned mainly through contact with patients: foreign sailors injured or taken ill during their visits to the busy port.

There was something about the letter, apart from the writer's obvious qualifications, which appealed to Edith. Her instinct for spotting the right, or wrong, nurse for her work had grown ever more acute during her years in Belgium, and here, she felt, was the sort of person she was looking for. She arranged an interview. What she saw and heard when she met Miss Wilkins only confirmed her first, spontaneous, reactions.

Elisabeth Wilkins and her younger sister had been orphaned early in life and brought up by their grandmother on the strictest Victorian lines, just as Edith had been. Like Edith, Elisabeth had found it no hardship: she was naturally serious, and felt no desire to "kick over the traces." During her training as a nurse she had not chafed at the restrictions and self-discipline; she was used to the former, and the latter came naturally to her. She enjoyed her work, and the feeling that she was doing something useful.

Listening to the yarns of the convalescing sailors (and if she had one weakness it was, on her own confession, that she "liked a good gossip") aroused only one longing in her — to travel: to see some of the faraway, colorful places the men talked about, and hear strange languages spoken. Miss Cavell's advertisement in the *Nursing Mirror* had, one day, turned what might have been just an idle dream into a real possibility. It was to be only a beginning, she promised herself excitedly as she sat in the train going back to Cardiff after her interview. Once she had had experience of working abroad, there was no end to the possibilities lying ahead. She might even work her way round the world!

It did not take Edith long to realize that her first impressions of Elisabeth Wilkins were correct. She was a first-rate nurse, and if anything, even stricter with the Belgian probationers than she was herself. Her coming lifted a great deal of weight off Edith's shoulders, but plenty remained. In addition to all her other work she was now responsible for watching over the building of the new Institute which was to replace the four houses in the rue de la Culture. This meant a daily visit to the building site; a constant watch to make sure that the new *Ecole belge d'Infirmières diplômées,* as it was impressively called, took shape exactly as she wished.

It was time she could ill afford, but it was time she loved. As she watched the walls slowly climbing upward she remembered her dream of — was it only five years ago? A dream of a big white hospital, shining with cleanliness; set in beautiful gardens; wards light and airy, painted in soft, bright colors — operating theaters equipped with every modern device . . . She could still hardly believe that here it was, actually growing before her eyes; visible proof of the success of her work.

Not that the way was completely smooth, even now. Although the steady flow of letters to Miss Lückes, asking for help and advice, had almost ceased a year after her arrival in Belgium, she did write one more, in the spring of 1913; a letter which spoke eloquently of the many disappointments and setbacks she had suffered during the years between:

> . . . Your letter braces me to fresh efforts in the good cause, and one needs that bracing here. The work is still very arduous and uphill. The spirit of the people is so opposed to the spirit of nursing. The young girls are brought up with no idea of duty and are selfish and too fond of pleasure. Miss Maude, Miss Evans and others have been sacrificed to the critical and narrow ideas of the people among whom they worked, and have been made the subject of slanderous gossip. I cannot tell you how much I have appreciated their work and efforts, and how grieved I am to think they should have been so hardly treated. We enlarge our borders and the "trained nurse" is making progress. All the new nursing homes and hospitals are engaging lay nurses and we have more demands than we can supply.
>
> The girls of the country come in very slowly and at present the school is cosmopolitan and at least half the pupils are foreigners.
>
> We have all the Board Schools under our supervision with twelve nurses at work in them, also a staff of twenty private nurses and our hospital, which I am thankful to say has made progress and

will, I hope, be a model in point of view of good
order, cleanliness and good nursing for the other
hospitals in Belgium.

My Committee are very good and kind and I
always feel to have their support in any difficulty.
They have the work much at heart and have raised
the necessary funds to build us a new school which
will be worthy of the object. We hope to be in-
stalled in about two years . . .

It was a letter eloquent as much for what it left out as
for what it included. Her bitterness here was all for friends
who had been ill-treated and unappreciated. She said
nothing of the jealousy and ill-will directed against herself.

From the beginning there had been those who resented
the "interference" of a foreigner in the nursing service of
Belgium and those who, while not actively hostile, would
gladly have seen the venture fail. Now that it was beyond
doubt proving to be a success there were ever increasing
murmurs that it was time a Belgian woman took over.
Petty criticisms were leveled at Edith, and no opportunity
was missed, by some, to point out the differences between
the Englishwoman and her Belgian colleagues, and the
misunderstandings which these gave rise to.

It seemed always the things she held most dear which
were the target for criticism: her dog, Jack; her friend and
protégée, Grace Jemmett.

Grace was a friend of Edith's younger sister Lilian and
her husband, Dr. Wainwright. During a long and serious
illness, during which she had been given frequent doses of

91

morphine, she had become addicted to the drug. She needed constant supervision and care, and Dr. Wainwright, thinking that Grace would stand more chance of complete recovery away from her indulgent family, and under the watchful eye of his sister-in-law, had asked Edith if she would accept the charge.

Filled with pity for the sad and almost desperate situation of someone still very young and lovely, Edith agreed; and very quickly Grace came to fill a blank in her life which had existed, without her realizing it, ever since she had left the François household nearly twenty years earlier. Always, until then, there had been happy children in her life. But during her nursing life there had been only the pale-faced children lying inert in hospital cots, seldom smiling, often indifferent to their surroundings. On them she had poured out her compassion and devotion, often to see them slip away like shadows.

At the St. Gilles Hospital she had devoted much of her time to the children's ward. She had had it decorated in blue and white, and put pictures on the walls to amuse her small patients. But they were still rarely more than that — for a few weeks or months they held up their arms in greeting when she came into the ward, and their faces lit with smiles. But a few days, or a few weeks later, they would be gone and other wan little faces would be on the pillows where they had rested.

She dared not allow herself to love any of them too much. But she needed someone to love, and Grace slipped easily and naturally into the empty corner of her heart. Although she was, in fact, in her twenties, there was something childlike about Grace which appealed to Edith's protective instinct and blinded her to the danger Grace was to the reputation of the rue de la Culture school. Edith was far more concerned with the pressing problem of fitting forty-eight hours' work into each day, and finding enough money to keep her school afloat — an experience she had first met during her short stay in Manchester six years earlier, and which had by now become a part of her daily life.

These were the problems she took to bed with her each night, and found waiting like venomous ghosts beside her pillow when she woke each morning. There was no escaping them — not even during her annual holiday; though then, for a little while, they lost their urgency.

These month-long breaks, spent with her mother in Norfolk, like her earlier visits to the country during her nursing training, enabled her to see her problems in perspective; as well as to rest, and meditate, and gather strength for another long year of battling against obstacles and difficulties.

Since her father's death in 1910, she and her mother had spent these holidays alone together, drawing always closer in understanding and love. For a little while Edith felt that she had not to be constantly on her guard. Some of the lines round her tired eyes smoothed out during these weeks of freedom from authority. Her lips more often curved upward in a grave smile, and her eyes lost their look of strain.

Even so, each year she arrived home in England looking more than a year older than last time, and in July 1914 it seemed to her mother that Edith was even slower than usual to throw off her worries. And as the days of July passed, more worries were added to those which concerned only her nursing work.

In an obscure little town in central Europe, the Archduke Ferdinand and his wife — heirs-apparent to the Austro-Hungarian throne, had been assassinated as they drove through the crowded streets. At first sight it seemed to have little to do with England — or Belgium — but a complicated system of treaties, guarantees and international agreements gradually revealed a delicately poised balance of power in Europe which made the situation an explosive one.

As she walked in the quiet, bee-haunted garden in Norwich, war seemed fantastically far away from Edith. It was a wonderful year for flowers, and the air about her seemed to shimmer with color and light. How could anyone think of violence amidst so much beauty? But the newspapers in her hand first whispered and, as the days went by, began to shout, that danger hung over the summer-heavy lands of Europe.

By the end of July there was no doubt in anyone's mind that conflict was about to break out and that, in her determination to overrun France, Germany was prepared to break the treaty which since 1839 had guaranteed Belgium's neutrality.

Louisa Cavell watched her daughter with sad and anxious eyes as the news grew graver. Her life had passed in an atmosphere of calm security — the only threats to her peace of mind the natural hazards of accident and illness, and a lack of sufficient money to give those she loved as much as she felt they deserved. This threat of war was something new, and terrible. The more terrible because she knew how inevitably, and deeply, her eldest daughter would be involved.

Without much hope she begged Edith to remain in England. There was so much she could do here at home. If England became involved in the war — and this seemed certain now — she would need every trained nurse available. Edith was much more than a trained nurse, and she was English. Her duty, surely, was to her own country first?

Edith shook her head sadly. Her duty was to her calling — to all mankind; and especially to those of mankind who needed her most. It was not merely a matter of countries, of patriotism. England had many brilliant and well-trained women in the nursing field. Belgium had so few — and would need those few so desperately during the months and years which lay ahead. There was no doubt at all in her mind where her duty lay, nor what she must do.

11

The sun shone down over Europe in a blaze of glory during the late summer of 1914; but it shone on chaos. News of the coming war caught people by surprise. Family parties on the beaches, wealthy travelers idling away the golden days in Continental resorts, businessmen thronging the busy streets of the capital cities, shook their heads at the rumors and smiled. It would pass, they thought with a careless shrug. Such things always did. Nothing really dreadful could happen while the sky was so blue.

But the rumors did not fade away, and in spite of the blue skies the clouds of war grew thicker and more menacing. The gossip in hotels and cafés took on a shriller note; voices sharpened with anxiety until at last, like a herd of wild deer scenting danger on the wind, the crowds of exiles rushed panic-stricken for the ports.

Standing on the crowded deck of the Channel steamer heading for Belgium, Edith felt torn almost in two. One home lay behind her, the other ahead. It had been an agony to leave her mother, whose brave smile had hidden nothing from the daughter who knew her so well. But her step did not falter as she battled her way along the quay at Ostend against the fear-driven people struggling to get on board the ship she had just left; and she did not cast even one wistful glance after the mob fighting for a place on board. England, much as she loved it, was behind her now. Her duty was to get back to Brussels as quickly as she could.

But that was more easily wished than done. Chaos had hit the Belgian railways too. Troops had to be transported, ammunition rushed to the frontiers, food stores assembled. Civilians must look after themselves. Useless to explain that Edith had a hospital to organize — no one had time to listen to a slight, gray-haired woman who spoke French with an English accent and who was therefore, presumably, asking awkward questions about how she was to get home, or safeguard her property in Belgium . . . Officials shook their heads, pointed vaguely first to this platform, then to another, muttered times of possible trains and hurried off before she could ask further questions.

It was Sunday, August 2nd, before she found herself, weary from an uncomfortable and protracted journey from the coast, in Brussels once more; and there was little rest for her there. The clinic must be prepared for the reception of wounded soldiers. Dr. Depage was absorbed in organizing a movable hospital to be set up close to the fighting lines, and the job of reorganizing the rue de la Culture clinic fell squarely on Edith. It was a job she shouldered gladly. It was good to be busy; to be doing something constructive; and it kept the nurses busy too. In them, fear was mingled with excitement — a mixture which threatened to be explosive unless they were kept occupied, as Edith very quickly discovered.

Several of the nurses in training were German, and they were dazed with fright at their position in a suddenly "hostile" country. The eyes of the Belgian nurses were full of resentment when they looked at them, and they were fearful of being trapped in what had become an alien land. Calmly Edith soothed their fears, helped them to pack their trunks, and took them down to the railway station. Her eyes were full of shadows as she watched them climb aboard the overcrowded train. It seemed impossible that, overnight, these girls she had watched over and taught could have become enemies.

It would only be for a little while, she comforted them. Quite soon the leaders of Europe would come to their senses, and the girls would be able to come back "home" and finish their training. But her heart was heavy as the train, packed with bewildered and terrified Germans, steamed slowly away.

Nobody, at first, believed that the war would last more than a few weeks, and the horrors and degradations it brought only gradually seeped into the consciousness of the people of Brussels as the weeks dragged into months, and the months into years.

Edith herself described vividly the slow change as the situation slipped from being almost a game into being one of grim reality when she wrote to the *Nursing Mirror* in the late Spring of 1915:

> On August 13th we had no conception that soon, and for many long, weary months, we were to be

virtual prisoners in the gay city of Brussels. Flags were hung from end to end, and no street, however mean, was without its stripes of orange, red and black. We were full of enthusiasm for the war, and full of confidence in the Allies. Crowds assembled everywhere to talk over the prospects of a speedy peace, and the newspapers published all day long, were sold in hundreds at every street corner. The sun shone and the glorious warm days of late summer were full of courage and anticipation. In the trams, in the trains, on the telephone one heard nothing but discussions on the situation. People who knew each other slightly, or not at all, waxed quite confidential in relating the latest news. We were chasing the spy, and preparing 18,000 beds for the wounded; all sorts and conditions of people were offering help, giving mattresses and blankets, rolling bandages, and making shirts; our chief thought was how to care for those who were sacrificing so much and facing death so bravely at Liège and elsewhere.

That was mid-August. It takes a great effort of the mind to go back and picture life as it was to us then.

After the period of high enthusiasm came the days of anxiety, growing keener hour by hour, when we heard Liège had fallen, that Namur had followed, and that the enemy was coming on in irresistible force. There were sinister tales, too, of burnt and battered houses, of villages razed to the ground, of women and children murdered, of looting and mutilation. And still we hoped against

99

hope. "We wait for England," was on the lips of everyone, and till the very last we thought the English troops were between us and the invading army.

It was a moment of heartbreak for the Belgian people when they realized that their hopes were in vain. Slowly their gay optimism dwindled, and the dreadful realization that the German army was sweeping forward invaded their minds, numbing their emotions and filling them with incredulity. Edith's "dispatch" goes on to describe how the last hopes fell as the Germans arrived at the gates of the city:

> Brussels lay that evening, breathless with anxiety. News came that the Belgians, worn out and weary, were unable to hold back the oncoming host who might be with us that night. Still we clung to the dwindling hope that the English army was between us and the unseen peril. For several days all the entrances to the town had been held by the Civil Guard, who had dug trenches and lay in them night and day, but it did not need a soldier to see that they could oppose no possible resistance to the great army of the Kaiser. It was a grateful duty to take these brave men hot coffee and food to fortify them against the nights, already chilly, of late summer.
>
> In the evening came the news that the enemy were at the gates. At midnight, bugles were blowing, summoning the Civil Guard to lay down their arms and leave the city. Many people were up

through the dark hours, and all doors and windows were tightly shut. As we went to bed our only consolation was the certainty that in God's good time, right and justice would prevail.

On August 20th the sun shone out in mockery on our fallen hopes; the last train left the capital at 6 A.M.; the rolling stock was shunted to Antwerp and the station closed. The King, the Royal Family, and the Government had left on the previous day, and the wireless apparatus connecting this little land with its big possession in Africa had been blown up. Many people left the city by motor, and crowds thronged the squares in front of the North Station, hoping for a chance to depart. All night long the wounded had been removed by ambulance to the station and sent away in safety to the last stronghold of Belgium. Later, we knew the city had been handed over to the enemy by its beloved Bourgmestre, M. Max — now a prisoner in Germany. In the afternoon, with much pomp and circumstance of war, the German troops marched into Brussels, and to the Town Hall, where the brave tricolour came down and the German stripes of black and white and red took its place. On the topmost spire still floated the Red Cross, which had been placed over all public buildings in which ambulances had been opened, to protect them. The Belgian crowd watched this desecration in silence and with profound sadness; some wept, but for the most part they showed great self-control, and no word of abuse or hatred escaped them. The police

101

moved about among them, exhorting them to calm and crying "Patience, patience."

The troops are all in grey, with their brass helmets covered and their arms of dull steel. There are at least twenty thousand who entered the city that day and camped in it for the night. Some were so terribly stiff that they could scarcely walk, and many had their feet sore and blistered with the long marching in heavy boots.

On August 21st many more troops came through; from our road we could see the long procession, and when the halt was called at mid-day and carts came up with supplies, some were too weary to eat, and slept on the pavement of the street. We were divided between pity for these poor fellows, far from their country and their people, suffering the weariness and fatigue of an arduous campaign, and hate of a cruel and vindictive foe bringing ruin and desolation on hundreds of happy homes and to a prosperous and peaceful land. Some of the Belgians spoke to the invaders in German, and found they were very vague as to their whereabouts, and imagined they were already in Paris; they were surprised to be speaking to Belgians and could not understand what quarrel they had with them. I saw several of the men pick up little children and give them chocolate or seat them on their horses, and some had tears in their eyes at the recollection of the little ones at home.

From that day till now, we have been cut off from the world outside — newspapers were first censored, then suppressed, and are now printed under German auspices; all coming from abroad were for a time forbidden, and now none are allowed from England. The telephone service was taken over by the enemy, and we were shortly deprived of its use. The post, too, was stopped, and, though now resumed to certain towns and countries, all letters must be left open and contain no news of war, or of anything of importance. The few trains that run for passengers are in German hands, and wherever you go you must have, and pay for, a passport. No bicycles are allowed, and practically no motors, so that once busy and bustling streets are very quiet and silent. So are the people, who were so gay and communicative in the summer. No-one speaks to his neighbour in the tram, for he may be a spy. Besides, what news is there to tell, and who has the heart to gossip, and what fashions are there to speak of, and who ever goes to a concert or a theatre nowadays, and who would care to tell of their all-absorbing anxiety as to how to make both ends meet and spin out the last of the savings or to keep the little mouths at home filled, with the stranger close by?

I am but a looker-on, after all, for it is not my country whose soil is desecrated and whose sacred places are laid waste. I can only feel the deep and tender pity of a friend within the gates, and observe with sympathy and admiration the high courage and self-control of a people enduring a long and terrible agony. They have grown thin and silent with the fearful strain. They walk about the city shoulder to shoulder with the foe and never see

103

them, or make a sign; only they leave the cafés which they frequent, and turn their backs to them, and live a long way off, and apart . . .

There was no doubt in anyone's mind now of the grimness of the situation, and its dangers. When the fall of Brussels seemed at last inevitable, Edith wrote to her family:

My darling Mother and Family,

If you open this, it will be because that which we fear now has happened, and Brussels has fallen into the hands of the enemy. They are very near now and it is doubtful if the Allied armies can stop them. We are prepared for the worst.

I have given dear Gracie and the Sisters a chance to go home, but none of them will leave. I appreciate their courage, and I want you to let the Jemmetts know that I did my best to send Gracie home, but she refused firmly to leave me — she is very quiet and brave.

I have nothing to leave but £160 in the Pension Fund, which has never been touched and is mine to leave. I wish mother to have it with my dearest love. It will supply the place of my little quarterly allowance to her.

If I can send my few jewels over, will you divide them between Flor and Lil, and please send Mrs McDonnell my long gold chain which she gave me, and a keepsake to Marion Hall?

I shall think of you to the last, and you may be sure we shall do our duty here and die as women of our race should die.

104

My dear, dear love to mother and Flor, Lil, Jack
Longworth and children; also to Evaline McDonnell. God bless you and keep you safe . . .*

Meanwhile, the people of Brussels settled down, after
the first shock, to a long, grim struggle. Temporarily
down, but far from defeated, they paused, incredulous that
such a disaster should have befallen them, and then gradually collected themselves and began to fight back. The
qualities they possessed which to Edith had at one time
seemed least desirable, in the new circumstances took on
new meaning: defiance of authority became a refusal to
buckle under their new "masters"; frivolity, at first crushed
by the overwhelming blow of defeat, returned in the form
of a laughter which lightened the day-to-day burdens and
humiliations; and the fierce independence which had sometimes been a trial in her nurses became a virtue as the enemy yoke grew heavier. It was a virtue which she herself
was to value, respect and share increasingly as the tide of
war rolled slowly, inexorably forward across the land that
she loved.

One of the few pleasures at this time was to play simple
practical jokes on the invaders, and the people of Brussels
became adept in tormenting their tormentors. Whole
streets of householders would enter into a conspiracy to
set their alarm clocks for a certain time in the evening,
when dusk was falling. The streets would empty, and the
patrolling guards — alerted by the unaccustomed stillness

* The letter never reached them. It was nearly twenty years
before the death of the German officer into whose hands it
had fallen revealed it to the world.

— would gather on the corners, rifles at the ready for an ambush. The sudden, wild clamor of bells sent them scattering, stumbling, calling contradictory orders until, as abruptly as they had started, the ringing bells were silenced, leaving the soldiers open-mouthed and foolish in the street, still empty but whose every window showed a mocking face.

A variant on this trick was to tie a heavy saucepan on the end of a cord and lower it with a crash onto the pavement behind a passing patrol, whipping it in through the window a split second before he turned and caught the culprit.

Punishment by curfew invariably followed, but to the inhabitants of Brussels such punishments were marked up as triumphs, for they were an unmistakable sign that the enemy's nerves were shaken, and every pinprick was a tiny wound in his armor.

But pinpricks were not enough. A more positive resistance was needed, and the opportunity for it came very soon.

12

SOME distance to the south and west of Brussels, on the French border, stretches the forest of Mormal: tranquil, leaf-shadowed and haunted by birdsong; inhabited, in the summer of 1914, only by a handful of foresters whose little houses, dotted about in the clearings, sent twists of blue-gray smoke among the branches, and whose axes made the only sounds to be heard, apart from the birds.

Peaceful villages clustered round the edge of the forest where early in the morning, as the villagers set out for the fields, the good scent of bread drifted out of the bakeries into the still air, and the contented clucking of chickens scratching about the cottage doorsteps mingled with the rattle of farm carts, the ring of heavy boots and the plodding of horses' hoofs.

It was holiday time. The children home from school for the long summer break gathered flowers in the meadows, as Edith Cavell had done in Norfolk forty years earlier. In the village of St. Waast-la-Vallée a young French schoolmistress, Louise Thuliez, was home from Lille for the holidays too, though with a heavier heart than usual. Rumors of war meant more, perhaps, to her than to some of her fellow villagers. Throughout her childhood her parents had told her stories of the Franco-Prussian war of 1870, and she had never forgotten them. Now war was threatening again. Desperately she told herself that these rumors were nothing new — that the threat would pass. Like the holiday makers she tried to believe that nothing evil could happen while the sun blazed down on the ripening harvest, but in her heart she knew that the harvest would never be gathered.

Then, on the 2nd of August the quiet of the little village was shattered by the wild ringing of bells — the signal that the worst had happened. Doors flew open, and little groups gathered in the dusty lanes, their eyes, wide and unbelieving, turned to the tower of the church which seemed to rock with the clamor of the bells. Hurrying figures in the distance left the fields of ripening grain and came running back to the village. Women flung themselves into the arms of their husbands and sons, and Louise Thuliez watched sadly, knowing that within a few days the families would be parted, and that many of them would never meet again.

The people of St. Waast-la-Vallée had little time for mourning their departed menfolk. Almost before they had recovered from the shock of the outbreak of war in Belgium, the advance guard of refugees and the retreating Allied armies came sweeping through the village, the haunting strains of the bagpipes adding poignancy to the pitiful procession. Farm carts piled high with family treasures mingled with the columns of weary soldiers. Children, clutching broken toys, their faces pale with fright at the memory of homes flaring like torches, stumbled dazedly beside the rumbling guns and ambulances filled with wounded men. Terror-stricken animals bleated, barked and neighed among the silently weeping peasants whose stupefied gaze was fixed on some far point towards which they hurried heedlessly, their only thought to put as great a distance as possible between themselves and the horrors they had left behind.

Evening brought an uneasy peace. The first wave of refugees had passed far beyond the village — driven remorselessly on by the fear of what lay behind and might be following. The summer-green hedges were thick with the dust of their passing and the ditches strewn with belongings which had fallen from the hastily packed carts: a wax doll smiled foolishly up at the darkening sky from the trampled grass of the roadside, a lidless saucepan caught the last rays of the dying sun; a dog with its paw crushed by a passing gun carriage howled agonizedly by a field gate.

Many of the cottage doors stood open, swinging in the gentle breeze, mute evidence that the inhabitants had joined in the headlong retreat. Only a handful of people remained in the village. As they gathered in the little square, talking in low tones, another convoy appeared — the remnants of an English regiment, many of them wounded, all of them exhausted to the point of collapse after three days of incessant fighting.

Beds were hastily made up for the wounded and the rest stretched out along the pavements of the village street to snatch a little sleep before pressing on. It was to be a brief respite, they knew, for the German army was hard on their heels.

The soft darkness of a summer night fell over the village. The soldiers slept uneasily, but the villagers lay awake, listening. Louise Thuliez, her eyes burning with weariness, turned restlessly on her pillow, her mind filled with tumultuous thoughts. Within a few days she had seen her beloved village stripped of its menfolk, deserted in terror by many of its families. Within the next few days — perhaps even hours — it would be at the mercy of the pitiless invaders.

She clenched her fist against the cool sheets as she remembered the white faces of the children; the wet, bewildered eyes of the old people who plodded through the village that day, their faces blank of hope. Their villages, too, lay deserted behind them — many of them in flames, pillaged and devastated. Unless the French people fought back with every weapon they possessed, the whole of France would follow, she thought bitterly. She could not join the army, as the men of St. Waast-la-Vallée had done. But there must be — there *would* be — some way she could fight for France's liberty, she vowed, staring at the small square of window beyond which, already, the sky was lightening.

Early the next morning the English regiment moved on. Ambulances came from the nearest Red Cross hospital to collect the wounded, but after they were filled, six men were left. The villagers were asked to care for them until the next morning, when the ambulances would return.

They never came back. By noon the same day the German army had reached St. Waast-la-Vallée.

For the next twelve hours Louise felt as if she was living in a nightmare. An endless river of gray uniforms swirled through the village. The air was loud with breaking glass and drunken, triumphant laughter, as the frugal villagers' stores of food were harvested by the invading army from cottages and shops. Gardens were trampled, hedges and fences broken down, livestock slaughtered. Terrified villagers were questioned, at gun-point, about the movements of the Allies who had left only that morning.

And then, when the village had yielded all it had to give, the gray, triumphant river swept on, southward and westward, into France, leaving behind it a trail of destruction, a tight little group of angry, humiliated villagers and — the six wounded English soldiers.

Nobody had attempted to conceal them from the invaders; knowing that it would be worse than useless. After the English regiment had left they had been moved into the house of Louise Thuliez's friend, Henriette Moriamé, and made comfortable in bed. Contemptuously, the Germans had left them there. They were, after all, only six in number and obviously (for they had torn off their blood-soaked bandages to be sure) of no danger. They could stay in St. Waast-la-Vallée for the present. There were more interesting, and more profitable, things to do than round up prisoners at the moment.

St. Waast-la-Vallée slipped back into a precarious peace, punctuated by regular visits from German ration wagons which depleted even further the villagers' scanty supplies of food. Nobody bothered with the wounded soldiers, so long as they were bedridden; but as the weeks crept by Louise and Henriette grew not less, but more, anxious. Under their care the wounds had healed; the men were stronger, and becoming restless with enforced inactivity. It would not be possible to keep up the pretense that they were still sick indefinitely. When that day came . . . both Louise and Henriette hated the thought of handing over to the Germans the six they had saved from that nightmare day in August.

At last the expected blow fell. Bills were posted throughout occupied France, announcing that all French or Allied soldiers must give themselves up as prisoners immediately at the nearest Town Hall. If they did not do so, the severest penalties would be inflicted not only on them, but on anyone giving them shelter.

There was only one thing to do. The six "guests" of St. Waast-la-Vallée must disappear.

Not far from the village stood the fairy-tale Château of Bellignies — home of the ancient de Cröy family where since the outbreak of war the delicate Princess Marie — cousin of half the nobility in Europe — had nursed the wounded of both armies with equal compassion and devotion while her brother, Prince Reginald, came and went on mysterious errands.

For the Prince and Princess the war was even more tragic than for their neighbors; to them it was a civil war, in which cousins faced each other across the battle line. But their hearts were with France, and it was to Prince Reginald, who knew every inch of the countryside and everyone in it, that Louise and Henriette turned for advice and help.

Two days later, as darkness fell, eight gray shadows slipped through a gap in the hedge that bordered the Moriamé garden and paused, listening. A dog whined uneasily in the lane close by and somewhere, a long way off, a cart rumbled. Then quietness fell and the Indian file of eight gray ghosts moved noiselessly away towards the forest of Mormal. A twig cracked; dry leaves rustled — a branch quivered . . . then there was silence.

Towards morning two gray ghosts returned to the village, as silently as they had left. As the sun came up over the forest, nothing stirred.

Later that day, Louise reported to the local mayor that the six English "prisoners" of St. Waast had escaped.

For the moment they were safe in their forest hide-out, but only for the moment. The countryside was alive with field-gray uniforms, and winter was coming on. Soon the kindly screen of leaves would be stripped from the trees by bitter winds, to reveal not one, but many hiding places; for Louise and Henriette quickly discovered, on their stealthy visits to "their" English soldiers, that the woods were full of others, left behind by the retreating Allied armies.

Like the forest animals they had crawled into holes, built themselves rough shelters of branches and twigs, and taken over deserted foresters' huts; and they waited, with nothing but blind hope to comfort them, for the moment when they could break through the encircling German army and rejoin their regiments.

113

It was a fragile hope, but it kindled an echoing glimmer in the girls' minds. With a kind of fierce joy they flung themselves into the task of feeding, clothing and watching over their disorganized little army. Though the short winter days held menace, the long dark nights offered cover for clandestine journeys. Louise learned to travel with no more noise than a blown leaf; to turn herself into a shadow at the sound of a cough, or a sudden movement. Together with Henriette she made friends in the villages that fringed the forest, and they found they were not alone in their self-imposed dangers. Behind the innocent façade of village life plots were being laid, messages carried, meetings and journeys arranged. In castle and cottage, presbytery and inn, social distinctions were laid aside and old enmities forgotten in face of the common desire to hit back at the enemy and keep the men in the forest free.

Louise found herself acting as go-between; from the forest she carried messages to the Château of Bellignies, between the thickness of whose massive walls other fugitives waited for the moment of escape; and from the Château back again to the forest she hurried with news and plans.

But as the weeks went by, in spite of their caution — in spite of the blank, "stupid" stares and shaken heads which greeted German inquiries — the obstinate refusal of the villagers to admit that there was anything alive in the forest except birds, German suspicions grew.

Frantically Louise and Henriette "covered up" behind the forest dwellers, who were not always as careful, themselves, as they might have been. Fires were doused at the merest whisper of wind through the undergrowth; lights

114

snuffed out at the creak of a branch. Even the blades of grass were carefully straightened to hide the passing of booted feet. But in vain. By mid-November reinforcements had arrived in the district. Gray uniforms and spiked helmets were everywhere.

The climax came one Sunday when, having been to Mass in a nearby village, Louise received a whispered warning from the parish priest.

"They're quartering the forest — searching it inch by inch," he told her in a low voice as they walked together through the churchyard. "We haven't much time."

"In case of alarm, strike camp and go to Bellignies." The emergency order thudded in Louise's ears as she crept stealthily through the forest, eyes and ears alert for warning sounds and movements. But — with thirty men! It was a tall order. She glanced at the sky through the leafless branches. Would the weather be kind? So much depended on that. She held out a hand, and a comfortingly heavy drop of rain fell, like a gift, into her palm. She sighed with relief. With luck, there would be no moon for an hour or so — and with a little more luck prowling sentries would keep within reach of shelter.

Nature was "kind." They struck camp to the patter of raindrops, and as they left the forest the black sky above seemed to open its sluice gates, tipping an icy deluge of water down onto the phantomlike procession. They reached Bellignies, soaked to the skin, but safe, at two o'clock in the morning.

As the two girls and tired men slept, Captain Preston, the senior English officer, held a council of war behind the shuttered windows of the Château. Was it, he asked gravely, fair that they should risk still further the lives of the two girls who had already risked so much? If, even now, they were to surrender . . .

But "No, no, no . . ." Louise and Henriette shook their heads vehemently when, the next morning, the suggestion was put to them. "To have risked so much, and then to have it wasted," Louise pleaded, "that would be far worse. All life is a risk these days. But this is a risk which could have a reward — if only we can save them."

There was, she went on eagerly, just a chance that a break through the lines could be made at a point on the railway on the far side of the forest. She and Henriette would go there that day and see how the land lay. If things looked good, the men could make a dash for it that same night.

"But that means walking thirty kilometers!" Captain Preston was aghast.

Louise nodded. "It will be worth it." She began to pull on her sodden shoes, worn thin as paper already from the many days and nights of tramping the lanes and forest paths. She looked at them anxiously. It would be a miracle if they lasted the day — but they were all she had. Shoes were not easy to come by since the German invasion.

Stiffly she got to her feet. "We will be back this evening," she said quietly. "By then we will know whether this escape route is possible."

The thin winter light was painting the Château gardens pewter-gray as they slipped through its imposing gateway. Captain Preston watched them unhappily as they melted away into the misty rain. So much could go wrong in the next few hours. One tiny slip . . . one careless word . . . . . . one little mistake in timing . . . With a sigh he turned from the window. It wasn't right, his conscience nagged him, that two girls should risk their lives like this.

The early winter darkness was down again before Louise and Henriette, stumbling a little and dazed with weariness, returned to Bellignies. But their faces, behind the weariness, were radiant. It could be done, Louise said jubilantly. It was a risk, of course, but thirty men — armed as they were, *could* break through.

The excitement died from her face at the sight of the grave faces around her. Apprehensively she looked round the little circle. "It *could* be done," she repeated, falteringly.

Captain Preston shook his head. "It has been decided," he said firmly, "that no more risks should fall on you and Mademoiselle Moriamé. It is not honorable of us to allow it. Tomorrow, we give ourselves up."

"*No!*" Louise's voice was sharp with anguish. "If you will not risk an open clash, take the men back to the forest. They could hide where the Germans have already searched. We — Henriette and I — will find food for them . . ." Her voice trailed away as the Captain shook his head, sorrowfully but decisively.

"It cannot go on," he said gently. "In your heart, you know it as well as I do."

With bitterness in her heart, Louise yielded, and with bitterness the next morning she watched the men gather together their few pathetic possessions and march away, on a journey which was to end in a prisoner-of-war camp in Germany.

Two days later, standing at her window in St. Waast-la-Vallée, she saw the vindication of Captain Preston's difficult decision. The rain no longer pelted its steel-tipped darts onto the sodden countryside. Instead the sky dropped, with menacing gentleness, flakes of snow as light as thistledown, which quickly coated every twig and branch and rooftop and spread, with deadly softness, a thick white carpet on which every footprint stood out clearly.

Captain Preston had been right . . . It could not have gone on. But the bitterness remained in Louise's heart. There would be no more surrenders, she promised herself. There were still men in hiding in the villages around Mormal. She would not rest until she had found other ways of saving them.

13

THE EIGHTEEN THOUSAND beds prepared in Brussels for wounded soldiers were never needed. So quickly did the tide of war engulf Belgium that the battle front was many miles to the southwest of the city before the dazed people of the capital had time to grasp the magnitude of the disaster which had struck them. But the work of the hospitals went on. Babies were still born, people fell sick; and even in the quiet streets, accidents still happened. The new school which was to replace the four houses in the rue de la Culture continued, slowly, to take shape. The clinic itself, the hospital of St. Gilles, and all the other hospitals over which Edith Cavell kept a watchful eye settled down to carry on with the work they had always done.

In some ways it was more difficult. There were shortages, and restrictions, and many things were "Verboten." But in other ways things became easier. War had convinced the women of Belgium, at last, that there was nothing dishonorable in hard work. Patriotism persuaded them, as Edith Cavell had been trying to do for so many years, that an aching back and roughened fingertips were things they could be proud of. They found, too, that work helped to keep at bay the nagging anxieties about husbands and sons; helped the dark days to go more quickly and gave them the sense of taking part, with their absent menfolk, in the struggle for freedom.

And yet, paradoxically, the work they did formed an oasis of neutrality in their war-torn world. In the wards and corridors of the hospitals and clinics of Brussels there were no "enemies"; only the sick and sorry who needed kindliness and help. Edith Cavell made sure that they received it. To her, a German soldier with a bullet wound was just as much in need of gentle nursing as a Belgian, or a French soldier, or a frightened refugee from a devastated village; just as much caught up in the great machine of war, and as hurt and puzzled by it. It was, she believed, her sacred duty to preserve life — any life, which was placed in her hands. Only God had the right to take that life away.

It was a belief which, very soon, came into conflict with her equally strong feeling for the absolute truth. There was no concealing the fact that among the patients in the Institute were a handful of wounded Belgian soldiers and, very soon, other Belgian men of military age suffering either from sickness or wounds. The German orders were that all such men, as soon as they were well enough, were to report to the nearest police headquarters. But that meant, as everyone well knew, deportation to Germany, and a prison camp; an end to freedom, perhaps even life itself, something that Edith could not contemplate.

Calling her nurses together she gave them clear instructions as to what they must do when a patient was ready to leave the clinic.

"You will explain to them," she said, "the route to the nearest German police headquarters — just as we have been ordered to do." She paused, and looked round at the nurses in the shocked silence which followed. "But then," she went on equably, "you will point out that if they take another route, it will bring them to the house of a friend who may be able to help them. If the German police then question you, you can honestly say that you directed the men to their headquarters. The men can decide for themselves which way they go."

A little sigh rippled round the tense group of listening nurses. Eyes brightened and heads nodded. They might have known that their clever Matron would find some way out of the difficulty. But their "clever Matron," left alone in her office, sighed and gazed out of the window, a crease between her brows. She was not as happy as her nurses about her plan, though it was the best she could think of to safeguard not only her patients, but the nurses themselves. She hoped they would not gossip about the arrangements. Brussels was full of listening ears.

If the nurses gossiped it was only among themselves. To the German police who questioned them, they presented innocent faces and wide-open eyes. It was quite true, they would admit cheerfully, that a number of patients had left the clinic only that morning — but of course they had instructed them to report to the police, as they had been told. Perhaps, being strangers in Brussels, the men had lost their way . . . ? There was nothing the German police could

121

do to prove that they were not speaking the truth. They went away, angry and frustrated.

And so, gradually, there sprang up throughout Brussels a network of people willing to take into their houses a Belgian soldier, still limping slightly, or with a scar across his face . . . an eighteen-year-old boy just recovered from pneumonia, but a "danger" to the German army because he was now old enough to fight for his country. There was no formal organization. No well-equipped network of trained resistance workers as, twenty-five years later, was to come into being during World War II. Each new recruit to the team constituted a risk to the rest, but it was a gamble they undertook gladly. It was the only way of striking back against the invaders, and if Belgium was to be set free the risk had to be taken.

Slowly, one by one, more and more of the citizens of Brussels were drawn into the fragile web of intrigue. A shopkeeper with an attic storeroom gave shelter for a night or two to an escaping soldier; a housewife foraging for her family carried a coded message in her basket among the loaves and cabbages; a schoolboy, bowling his hoop innocently along the pavement, carried word that a guide was waiting at a certain place to lead a group of refugees to safety beyond the city limits.

It was only a matter of time before the underground movement in Brussels linked up with that on the French border to the southwest. There Louise Thuliez and Henriette Moriamé were not alone in their rescue work. Among others Hermann Capiau, a mining engineer from the Black Country of Belgium, and the Countess de Belleville, an old friend of the de Cröys, had from the earliest days played their part as links in a chain that led to the Dutch border and freedom for many an Allied soldier.

It was through Monsieur Capiau that Edith Cavell became, not merely one link in that chain, but the strongest and most important of all. November 1st, 1914, was the fateful day on which her destiny was decided. A friend of Monsieur Capiau — a barrister named Libiez — had for some time been hiding an English officer and a sergeant when news came that a German house-to-house search was being made in the district. Knowing of Monsieur Capiau's underground work, he asked him to help the two Englishmen to escape.

The route by which Monsieur Capiau had been crossing the Dutch frontier had been closed, following the fall of Antwerp, and the only possible way now seemed to lie through Brussels.

It was a hazardous journey, and the three men did not reach the city until dusk was beginning to fall. In a few hours curfew would be upon them, and the streets deserted except for patrolling German soldiers. Anxiously Monsieur Capiau set out on a round of slender "contacts." One was away, guiding a party to the frontier; another had been shot and wounded by a sentry on his last trip. A third was out — nobody knew where. A fourth house was full already of men waiting for escorts to safety.

Desperately Monsieur Capiau racked his brains for more reliable names. "Try Madame Depage, the doctor's wife — she might be able to help," advised the man whose house was already full.

Leaving the two Englishmen in temporary shelter Monsieur Capiau slipped into the dark street. It was a last hope. He knew no one else in Brussels whom he could trust. The sound of measured footsteps made him freeze in the shadows. A sentry passed, banging his hands together in the frosty air and muttering complaints. Monsieur Capiau held his breath until he had gone by, then darted down the street in the direction of the address he had just been given.

His heart sank when, a quarter of an hour later, the doctor's wife shook her head regretfully. "I have my children to think of," she explained gently. "My own life is not so important — but I cannot risk theirs." She paused. "You say these men are English?" Monsieur Capiau nodded. Madame Depage looked thoughtful. "Then I think perhaps I can help after all." She pulled a piece of paper towards her on the desk before which she was sitting. "Go to this address . . . it is a nursing home. The Matron there is English. I feel sure she will not refuse to shelter two of her countrymen."

Monsieur Capiau looked at the envelope into which she had thrust the note. "149 rue de la Culture — Mlle. Cavell," he read.

14

"THERE'S someone to see you, Matron." Edith Cavell looked up to see Sister Wilkins standing uncertainly in the doorway of her office.

"At this time of night, Sister?" She raised her eyebrows. "Who is it?"

"He wouldn't say. Just that he wanted to see you, and that it was urgent."

"Very well, ask him to come in." Edith closed the account book on her desk and stood up, smoothing the dark blue material of her dress. It was late for a German inquiry, but surely no one else would be abroad at such an hour? Had one of her nurses been indiscreet? Or had one of the patients grown overbold on leaving the clinic, and fallen into enemy hands? The door opened, and she felt a momentary spasm of relief. Her visitor was not a German, of that she felt sure.

"Mademoiselle Cavell?" he asked, hesitating in the door-way.

She nodded. "I am the Matron here. What can I do for you?" Silently Monsieur Capiau held out the note Madame Depage had written. Silently Edith took it, recognizing the writing on the envelope with surprise. As she read, Monsieur Capiau was aware of the sounds beyond the quiet room: the subdued clatter and murmur of voices — the sounds of a well-run hospital settling down for the night. It would be a perfect hiding place. If only he could leave his two fugitives here for a little while.

Nurse Cavell looked up. "Who are these men?" she asked.

"Colonel Bodger, of the 8th Cheshire Regiment, and Sergeant Meachins. They were stranded after the retreat from Mons. A friend of mine has been hiding them, but it has become too dangerous, for him and for them. The Colonel was wounded, and needs treatment. If only you could have them here for a little while, until he is well, and arrangements can be made to smuggle them over the frontier . . ."

He waited anxiously while the grave-faced woman in front of him smoothed the letter in her hand. At the mention of the Colonel's injuries she looked up quickly.

"Is he badly hurt?"

"He is recovering, but the journey into Brussels didn't help him, and if the Germans discover that he and the Sergeant have been hiding, after the order to surrender, things might go very badly for them."

"Bring them here. We will take care of him until he is well. After that . . ." Nurse Cavell spoke with sudden decision. "After that we will see. We have many friends in Brussels. Perhaps they will be able to help them cross the frontier." Before Monsieur Capiau could break in with

126

eager thanks she went on. "You will be careful? I have my nurses to think of."

"Of course. There are many people involved already. We will take no chances."

After he had gone, Edith stood for a long time looking down at Madame Depage's letter. Then, with a sigh, she tore it across once, twice, three times. After a moment's hesitation she took a box of matches from her pocket and set fire to one corner of the scraps of paper and watched them flare up. As she dropped the curls of black ash into the fireplace she sighed again. The world in which she had lived for almost fifty years — a black-and-white world of right and wrong — seemed to have flared up and died with her friend's letter, leaving her in a bewildering new world where the ground shifted under her feet and truth and right had become tinged with the gray of dishonesty and evasion.

But how could she turn away men who were ill, and in danger? All her nursing instincts cried out against such an act of callousness. And if she were careful, the need to lie about their presence might never arise. It would only be for a few days. After that they would be safe, and her conscience would be at rest.

Calmly she glanced at a plan of the clinic. There was an empty room on the top floor of the house where she had her office. The men would be secure there for a day or two. After that, she repeated to herself, they would be someone else's responsibility.

She reckoned without Monsieur Capiau and the underground movement which centered on the Mormal district.

127

German surveillance of the area had tightened with the surrender of the men from the forest, and it became obvious that any fugitives left in the area were in imminent danger of discovery. It was vital that they should be smuggled away as quickly as possible. The country between Mormal and the Dutch border was alive with troops and the only way left was northeast, across the French border to Brussels. Here there was just a hope that the fleeing soldiers could mingle with the crowds and find a brief refuge in one of the many friendly houses of the loyal Brussels citizens until guides could be found to take them to the frontier.

Shortly after Colonel Bodger and Sergeant Meachins had been safely smuggled out of Belgium, Monsieur Capiau arrived again in Nurse Cavell's office. She had been kind enough to help him once — would she do so again? It was desperately urgent. She listened to him in silence. By now the fugitive soldiers were more than a heart-stirring abstraction; no longer faceless, and voiceless. Sergeant Meachin's rough thanks and the clasp of Colonel Bodger's thin hand in hers were still vivid in her memory. Whatever the cost to herself or her conscience, she could not be deaf to other cries for help.

"Bring them to me," she said quietly. "As soon as they are fit to travel I will make arrangements for them to go."

Shortly afterwards she had another visitor: Prince Reginald de Cröy. He and his sister, he explained, were too well known to guide men into Brussels, but they had worked out a system whereby the men could travel the last part of the journey by trolley car, armed with false papers prepared by himself and containing photographs taken by the Princess with a camera she had managed to hide from the Germans. Monsieur Capiau had told him of Nurse Cavell's generous help with Colonel Bodger and Sergeant Meachins. Would she help him too? If she agreed, he would direct the men to her nursing home . . . she would recognize them by the password "Yorc," which was his own name in reverse.

What else could she do?

In February 1915, Louise Thuliez herself called at 149 rue de la Culture, and the circle was complete. Edith Cavell was committed to the work of rescue which was to save so many lives.

It was, as Monsieur Capiau told her, becoming ever more urgent. The Germans were angered, not only by the knowledge that their enemies were slipping through their fingers but by the growing impudence of the Belgian resistance. A secret newspaper, *La Libre Belgique,* had begun to make its appearance in letterboxes and among the morning mail delivered not only to loyal Belgians, but the Germans themselves. Even the German Governor General, Baron von Bissing, received a weekly copy — and all the efforts of the police and the army to discover the origins of the paper and its distributors failed dismally. It seemed to appear out of nowhere, like a conjuror's rabbit, and its smudged title, mocking the Governor General from among official papers on his desk, sent him into a frenzy of frustrated rage one day out of every seven each week. A contingent of the crack Secret Police was sent down from Berlin and discipline everywhere in Brussels was tightened, but still the secret remained.

All through that early spring tension mounted, and with it the danger. More and more men were creeping out of hiding in the woods and villages of northern France as the "jungle telegraph" spread the news of successful escapes and the people of France and Belgium scoured the countryside for hidden troops. Louise Thuliez walked for miles through the sodden woods and fields, seeking news of refugees from the German army.

In her small, austere office in the rue de la Culture Edith Cavell, white-haired now and as light and fragile as a winter-withered leaf, battled daily not only with the routine difficulties of running a hospital in wartime, but with the mounting bills for food and medicines which could never be paid for by the men who needed them. Every spare corner of the clinic was taken up with "patients" who not only constituted a constant danger but whose hearty appetites stretched the slender resources of the Institute to the cracking point.

There were other strains on the funds too — the men often needed clothes by way of disguise when they left Brussels, and a little money in their pockets for carfares out of the city. Those who could not be housed in the clinic had to be found shelter elsewhere, and the kind people of Brussels who gave them protection often turned to her for help in buying food.

The columns of figures in the shabby account books grew longer and more alarming as the weeks went by.

130

Was it right, Edith asked herself, to spend the money of the Nursing School in this way? But what other way was there? The men must be fed; the guides who took them to the frontier must be paid. If only she had someone to consult . . . But Dr. Depage and his wife Marie were far away, busy with their mobile hospital near the front lines by now, and there was no one else she felt she could turn to. Sister Wilkins, loyal and sympathetic though she always was, had no authority to comfort her where matters of hospital administration were concerned.

She had almost forgotten what it was like to talk on equal terms about the business of the school when one day to her great joy José, the Rumanian houseboy, knocked on her office door and told her that Madame Depage had called to see her.

It was only a few months since they had parted, but it seemed like a lifetime: so much had happened, to them and their beloved Belgium. The Clinic in the rue de la Culture was not the only organization to be short of funds. Poor Belgium had been drained of all her riches, and everywhere everyone was becoming desperate for food and fuel. Electricity and gas had been cut off, and even water was restricted. All the hospitals were short of equipment, drugs and medicines. That was the reason for her visit, Marie Depage explained. She had decided to make the perilous journey across the Atlantic to America, to appeal for help. She would be away for several months, but if all went well, she should bring good news back with her; and more than that — money which would help them all to carry on the work they were doing.

It was a relief for Edith to be able to share some of her worries about the financing of the Nursing School with her old friend, and to receive the assurance that Dr. De-page would never blame her for using the money entrusted to her to help escaping soldiers. A relief, too, to know that sometime in the near future financial help might be coming, so that the work of the hospitals would not suffer because of the work she was doing for the underground movement.

But mixed with her relief was a sense of loss when Madame Depage left her. Although they had not been able to meet very often during the months of war, the sense of separation was even greater now that Edith knew that her friend was leaving the country. Dr. Depage was far too busy to have time to bother with the Nursing School and in any case, there had never been a great bond of sympathy between them as there had been between Edith and Marie Depage. The Ladies' Committee, too, had far more to occupy themselves with now than in peacetime, and even those who were still closely connected with the school often disapproved of its connection with the escape work. It was not fitting, they felt, that the Matron of the Nursing Home should take part in such dangerous activities. If ever the Germans were to discover the use to which the clinic was being put, it might be disastrous.

Edith herself was aware of this, and unhappy about it, but now that she was committed, there was no going back. The stream of English fugitives was slowing down, but French and Belgian men of military age were on the run from forced labor and the prison camp. How could she, when she had helped so many of her own countrymen, refuse to help them too?

Slowly the solid wall of trust and respect she had built around herself during the seven long years in Brussels seemed to be crumbling away. Her colleagues now were the mercurial birds-of-passage who came by night, stealthily, and as stealthily left; the loyalist people of Brussels in whose houses her protégés found sanctuary, and the hard core of underground workers: Louise Thuliez, Prince Reginald de Cröy, Hermann Capiau and Philippe Baucq, a young Brussels architect who was largely responsible for the distribution of *La Libre Belgique*.

Thinking of these things, there was a great sadness in her heart as she sat alone on the evening after Marie Depage had left her. For an hour or two she had felt close to someone who understood her. It had been like drinking deeply at a clear well, after weeks of traveling through an arid desert. She could not hope for such refreshment for many more months to come.

In fact, summer was beginning to dust the trees with green, and bring a life-giving warmth to the chilled air of Brussels when she learned that she had turned for the last time for sympathy to the doctor's understanding wife. Anxious to return as quickly as possible to Belgium after her successful tour of America, Marie Depage had booked a passage on the fast Cunard liner *Lusitania*. She almost looked forward to the voyage. She had done well in America; she was coming home with money in her pocket, and many more promises of help. Summer was coming, and things would be easier for the poor people of her beleaguered Belgium.

But summer had brought out the hunting packs of submarines in the Atlantic, too. Within sight of the Irish coast the *Lusitania* was torpedoed and sunk. Nearly twelve hundred people went down with her. One of them was Marie Depage.

The news was broken to Edith as soon as it arrived in Belgium. After she had heard it she became, to her nurses, an even more remote and withdrawn figure. She remained always kind and gentle, thoughtful for others and sensitive to their needs, but she herself was unreachable. Only Sister Wilkins, loving and understanding her more than most, could get near to her and even she felt the wall of reserve shutting her out from full companionship. Edith Cavell had always been a single-minded person, with a strong driving force urging her on to do the work she felt she was born to do: now that work crystallized, for her, into the necessity for defending, almost singlehanded, a growing army of wanted men.

The men themselves were not always as helpful as they might have been. After living in attics and cupboards, cellars and holes in the ground, the sight of a city even as war-stricken as Brussels went to their heads. Freedom was within their grasp, after months of living like animals. It was impossible to subdue their high spirits, or persuade them that their sense of security was illusory. If they could get away from the guard-infested fields and forests of Mormal without detection, who was going to spot them among the Brussels crowds? The Germans were obviously fools — and the whole of the Belgian people were on their side.

Helplessly, Edith watched them swaggering about the streets of the city, apparently oblivious of the danger they brought not only to themselves, but to her and her friends and nurses. But she refused to "imprison" them in the clinic while they were waiting for the guides to smuggle them away. They had been prisoners long enough already.

People were beginning to talk. In the wine shop near the clinic English soldiers had been seen drinking with Belgian workmen from the district, and they had also been seen — and heard — returning to the School of Nursing in the rue de la Culture. Eyebrows were raised, and voices lowered — but not quite enough. Groups of "workmen" began to appear in the road opposite the clinic, who did very little work. They seemed more interested in what was going on in the nursing home than in the rather vague job on which they were engaged. The nurses, going to and fro in the street, glanced nervously at them, and turned away quickly, almost guiltily, from their shrewd, appraising stares.

Anxiously, Sister Wilkins begged her Matron to take more care. But Nurse Cavell only shook her head. So long as there were men in hiding, she would help them. Nor did she even wait, now, for them to be brought by people she could trust. Whoever turned up on her doorstep with a plea for sanctuary was accepted. Brussels was full of rumors that prisoners were being shot out of hand by the Germans. It was better, she felt, to accept someone who

135

might be a potential source of danger than to turn away someone who desperately needed help.

And that some of their refugees *were* sources of danger Sister Wilkins did not doubt. Even those who arrived under the protection of people they knew sometimes made her feel uneasy. Gaston Quien was one of them. The Prince de Cröy brought him one day in early summer, and from the moment he crossed the threshold, Elisabeth Wilkins felt the pricklings of suspicion. She tried to tell herself that it was her Victorian upbringing and natural sedateness which made her dislike the tall Frenchman whom the other nurses so quickly came to adore. But . . . there was something about his eyes, and the mocking twist to his lips. His anxiety to be liked and trusted only strengthened her suspicions. She tried not to feel this way. Matron seemed quite happy about him; she even lent him money from the tiny hoarde which was growing more slender every month. Why, then, should she have this feeling of uneasiness? She wished he would leave, quickly. The companion who had arrived with him left the next day, but Quien lingered. He did not feel well, he pleaded. The strain of enforced captivity . . . He had never been strong . . . The journey to the frontier would be too much for him until he felt better.

And so he stayed on, and on. Wheedling small sums of money out of Nurse Cavell, flirting with the nurses, alternately charming and exasperating everyone except Sister Wilkins. Between the two of them stretched a thin, taut wire of suspicion, dangerous as a coiled snake.

One afternoon, Elisabeth called in at her Matron's office

to discuss some small problem which had arisen on the wards. While they were talking a knock came on the door. A moment later Quien's face, smiling ingratiatingly, appeared. His hands were behind his back in the coy gesture of someone hiding a surprise. Tilting his head on one side his smiling glance went from Matron Cavell's face to Sister Wilkin's. He held the latter's eyes for a moment in challenge. Then he whipped his hands from behind his back. In each he held a large, brightly colored bouquet of flowers.

"A token of gratitude for the kind ladies whose house has become my home." He bowed. There was a moment's astonished silence. Then Nurse Cavell stretched out her hand for the flowers.

"How . . . how kind," she murmured. There was a faint flush on her cheeks, but her eyes were inscrutable.

"And Sister?" Quien held out the other bunch of flowers, his eyes wary and questioning. Slowly Sister Wilkins took the flowers. "Thank you." Her voice was expressionless.

After the door had closed behind Quien, Nurse Cavell turned to her companion with a sigh. "I can think of ways in which the money might have been more usefully spent," she remarked wryly.

Sister Wilkins said nothing. She put down the flowers on the table nearby and surreptitiously wiped her hand on her skirt.

"Perhaps it *is* time he went," Nurse Cavell admitted. "I will make arrangements this evening. He must be made to see that he cannot stay here indefinitely."

Sister Wilkins's heart lightened when Quien, protesting,

was firmly directed to join the next band crossing the border. For a few days she felt almost safe. The work could not go on much longer, she told herself. An end must come to the stream of refugees. The front line was now many miles from Brussels, and the stragglers left behind by the early battles had almost all been captured, or escaped. Soon — quite soon — they would be able to settle down to the routine of caring for the sick and training young nurses. Life would be far from easy, but at least they would not be living eternally on the edge of a crumbling precipice.

Her mood of optimism was short-lived. In less than a week, Quien was back on the doorstep of 149 rue de la Culture. Aghast, Sister Wilkins learned the news from her Matron.

"He says that French officials in Holland have given him money to return, to do Intelligence work," she explained.

"I don't believe it. I think he's a spy."

Nurse Cavell looked sharply at her young lieutenant. "Perhaps it would be better if we took no further chances," she said slowly, reluctantly. Sister Wilkins breathed a sigh of relief. But she remained uneasy. Quien had seen so much of what was going on in the clinic. If her suspicions were soundly based he had seen more than enough to condemn her Matron in the eyes of the Germans. And if he were a spy, how were they to know that there were not others among the motley collection of men who had taken shelter under their roof? She found herself looking at the men with new eyes; listening more carefully to their conversations — watching their movements. Each time a new batch left for the frontier she sent up a little prayer of thankfulness.

Then, one day when she was tidying up the rooms after one such group had left, she found on the floor of a cupboard a heap of torn-up scraps of paper. Trembling, she gathered them up and took them to Matron's office.

"He was trying to hide something, Matron. Why should he hide anything from us, we were trying to help him?" she asked.

They both looked down at the torn scraps of paper scattered across Nurse Cavell's desk. The pieces were too small for them to read what was written on them.

"Perhaps the letters were personal ones which he felt were for no eyes but his." Edith's voice did not hold much conviction, but she smiled comfortingly. "Try not to worry so much, Sister. We are beginning to see danger where perhaps it does not exist."

But Elisabeth was not to be comforted so easily. "Please, Matron — haven't you done enough? Those workmen out in the roadway . . . They aren't really doing a job. They just watch us, all the time. They know what is going on here. Isn't it time to stop?"

Sadly, Nurse Cavell shook her head. "It's too late, my dear. Of course the Germans must know what we are doing. But if we are arrested we shall be punished in any case, whether we have done much or little, so let us go ahead and save as many as possible of these unhappy men."

15

SISTER — there's someone to see you." The scared voice of one of the younger nurses at the door of a patient's room made Sister Wilkins turn, a little guiltily. Matron was spending the morning at the new nursing school and had left her in charge. She had paused in her rounds to chat with the four Belgians who were waiting for an escort to the frontier where they hoped to join an Allied regiment. It was not, perhaps, the most dignified moment for her to be discovered by a junior member of the staff. But she quickly recovered her poise.

"Very well, Nurse — I'm coming."

She followed the little nurse out of the room. "Who is it?"

"I don't know. I've never seen him before."

Sister Wilkins hurried down the stairs. A man was waiting inside the front door; someone she did not recognize. His back was to the light and his face half in shadow.

"What can I do for you?" she asked.

"Have you any more left?" The question was abrupt, but spoken in fluent French. Sister Wilkins felt a moment of exasperation. That the man had come from one of the other Brussels hospitals in search of well-trained nurses, she never doubted. It was a regular feature of the school's life. Hardly a day passed without some call being made on them, and their own staff had dwindled to a point where there were hardly enough nurses to keep the clinic running smoothly.

"No one," she answered a little shortly. The line must be drawn somewhere!

There was a pause. Then: "What, no more Tommies?" The man's voice was almost silky. Sister Wilkins looked up sharply. "What do you mean?" She hoped the quaver she felt in her throat did not sound in her voice.

The man raised his hand and lifted the lapel of his coat. Under it she saw the dull gleam of a badge: the badge of the German Secret Police. Under her feet the floor seemed to dissolve, then steady.

"I don't know what you are talking about," she said quietly.

"No?"

"No." Her voice was quite firm now. "But if you have anything to discuss with me, you had better come to my room next door."

After a moment's hesitation the man followed her out into the street. Sister Wilkins's mind was quite clear now. She must, somehow, keep him out of the house they had just left. Luckily the four Belgians were the only refugees on the premises at the moment. Two Englishmen had left the previous night. If she could get a message to José, the houseboy, he would be able to smuggle them out to a place

141

of safety. She climbed the stairs to her room slowly. Time was the most essential factor. She must keep him busy talking until she found some way of getting the message through. In her room she turned and faced the stranger.

"Now, what is it you want?"

"You know perfectly well. You have been hiding enemy soldiers and Belgian men of military age. It is an open secret in the town. Did you think we knew nothing of it? Do you think the German Secret Police so stupid?"

"I don't know what you are talking about. I know nothing about the soldiers you speak of." Elisabeth closed her fingers round the edge of her desk for support. "You may search this room if you wish. I have nothing to hide."

The German looked round. The sitting room was small and neat. Papers were stacked on the desk at the Sister's back. If she was so willing for him to search them there was probably nothing worth finding, but on the other hand she might be bluffing. Brusquely he brushed her aside and began to riffle through the piles of paper. He grunted as he came to the last one.

"I told you there was nothing," Sister Wilkins pointed out.

"You have men here, in this hospital," the German persisted.

"Certainly — there are several patients in the men's ward. Do you wish to see them?"

The man nodded, flashing a suspicious look at her innocent face. But his confidence was waning. Perhaps, after all, he had made a mistake. This young woman was far

142

too calm for someone who was risking if not death, then a long term of imprisonment.

In the men's ward he questioned the patients gruffly, and examined their papers. Behind his back Sister Wilkins signaled to one of the nurses on duty. The girl, already a little alarmed by the sight of what was obviously an official investigation, approached uncertainly.

"German," Sister Wilkins mouthed urgently. "Tell José."

The young nurse's eyes widened with fright, but a second later she had pulled herself together. As she slipped from the ward Sister Wilkins turned back to the German policeman, her face bland and impassive.

"You are satisfied?" she asked. "There are more patients on the other side of the ward. Perhaps you would like to question them too. Though I would remind you that this is a hospital. Many of the men are very sick — it is bad for them to be upset. I should be glad if you would keep your questioning to the minimum."

"It is their papers I wish to see," snapped the German. "Papers tell more than people these days, you know. I wish to see *all* the hospital papers."

Elisabeth felt suddenly cold. She was a fool to believe that he would be satisfied with a visit to her room, and one ward. Nurse Cavell's room could hardly expect to escape inspection, and there were enough incriminating documents there to send Matron to prison for life. Somehow she must find a way of slipping out of the ward for a few moments. But how?

143

Behind her the door opened and closed. The young nurse who had been sent on the errand to José was back, her face wreathed in smiles. As she caught Sister Wilkins's eye her own left eyelid quivered triumphantly. She was beginning to enjoy the conspiracy. With a saucy swing of her starched skirts she flounced round the end of the bed next to the one where the German was standing, picked up a thermometer, flicked it deftly and popped it between the lips of the startled patient.

"Work must go on, mustn't it, Sister?" she said brightly and, turning her shoulder casually to the German: "All's well," she signaled across the bed to Sister Wilkins.

"Work must go on . . ." Elisabeth clutched at the straw. "Indeed it must, Nurse," she replied. Then, with a meaning look: "Has the patient in Room 24 had her treatment yet?"

"In Room . . . ?" For a second the nurse looked puzzled and then, meeting the plea in Sister Wilkins's eyes, she recovered. "Not yet, Sister. She's waiting for you now."

"You must excuse me." Sister Wilkins turned to the German. "You will understand that the work of a hospital goes on unceasingly. If you wish to see me again when you have completed your investigation, Nurse will bring you to me."

Without waiting for his assent she slipped out of the room. On trembling legs she ran up the stairs to Matron's office. There would be no time to destroy anything, but with luck the most incriminating documents could be hidden.

144

With shaking fingers she turned over the papers on Edith's desk. The most innocent she scattered about, the rest she bundled together. Then she looked round — no use hiding them in there; it was the most likely place for a thorough search. With her heart in her throat she stepped out on to the bare landing. Nothing there except a lavatory. No cupboards, no . . . The lavatory! Quickly she whipped open the door. Above her head the cistern gurgled. A chair stood against the wall. There was a plop, a subdued clank as she replaced the cover on the cistern. The next moment she was walking sedately down the stairs. Halfway down she met the German policeman and the nurse from the men's ward. He looked at her suspiciously.

"Where is the Matron's room?" he asked brusquely. Serenely Sister Wilkins turned and led him up the stairs. In Nurse Cavell's office she stood with folded hands while he turned over the papers on the desk. Then with a final grunt he turned and walked past her to the door.

"Don't imagine that I'm satisfied," was his parting shot as he went down the stairs. Sister Wilkins sank into the nearest chair, sick with relief.

When she returned an hour later, Nurse Cavell listened impassively to the story she had to tell.

"José managed to get the four Belgians out to Madame X. They hadn't even time to dress properly. Monsieur B. was still wearing his bedroom slippers. But they're safe for the present. We *must* destroy the books and papers though. The Germans will be back again, I'm sure," Elisabeth pleaded. Nurse Cavell nodded her agreement. "And

145

please, Matron, please don't have any more of the men here. It's too dangerous. We know now that *they* know, and they'll never give up until they catch you."

A few days later Nurse Cavell had an early-morning visitor. It was the first time that she and the Princess de Cröy had met, though for months now they had both been working on the same mission. Edith had been attending an operation in the theater when she arrived and found her waiting in the office. The Princess turned from the window as she entered, and made a nervous little gesture of conciliation towards Jack as he bounded up to her exuberantly.

"He won't hurt you," Edith assured her with a ghost of a smile. "But I wish you hadn't come here. I'm afraid I'm under suspicion. Those men you see through the window have been there for some time now. They do very little work, but seem most interested in all that goes on in this house. And twice this week the German police have called and searched the buildings. Luckily I was able to destroy such evidence as I had on paper and they went away, but we might not always be so lucky."

The Princess sighed. "In any case the work must stop. We too have had search parties at the Château. We dare not take any more men to Bellignies."

"Are there any more men hidden?"

The Princess hesitated and then, reluctantly, she said: "Mademoiselle Thuliez found more than thirty in hiding in Cambrai only a day or so ago."

Nurse Cavell straightened her back and lifted her chin. "Then we cannot stop, can we?" she said steadily. "If only one of those men was caught, and shot, we would be to blame for his death."

"But if he is hidden here, or at Bellignies, we might bring about just what we are trying to prevent," the Princess pointed out.

"Then we must find other hiding places for them. I can still arrange for guides, and make sure that they are fed and clothed, and that those who are injured receive proper treatment."

"It is getting more difficult for them to cross the frontier," the Princess went on worriedly. "In the early days it was possible to bribe the guards, but now . . ."

Edith nodded. "They are using electric wires, too. Our guides from Brussels are clever — they managed to overcome this by using barrels for the men to creep through, but even so there have been . . . accidents. Guides are becoming more and more scarce. Even Philippe Baucq has insisted on leading several groups recently. I begged him not to — he has his wife and children to think of, and so much other valuable work to do, but he would not listen to me. I think I can understand. For months now he has watched other young men go off on this dangerous work, and many of them have not returned. He feels he cannot any longer refuse to share the risks they are taking. But I am worried about him."

The two women looked at each other for a moment in silence; their unspoken thoughts about so many brave Belgian and French patriots hanging in the air between them.

147

"We must take no risks that might bring suspicion on others," Edith went on at last. "Those of us who are deeply involved must meet as seldom as possible, and take every care that we are not followed." She paused and smiled, one of her rare, sweet smiles. "What I am to say now will, I'm afraid, seem melodramatic, but unfortunately we live in melodramatic times . . . When you leave this house I want you to walk to the end of the road. In front of you, you will see a shop window which reflects the road behind you. When you see that no one is following you, turn quickly down the road to the left. There is a pastry cook's shop just by the trolley stop. Stand looking in the window, as if you intended to buy something, until you hear the bell announcing that a car is just about to leave. Then jump on it quickly, so that there is no time for anyone to follow you . . . Don't bother which way it is going. The important thing is that you should get away from here as soon as you can — and without anyone seeing where you are going."

It was, as she said, a plan which might have come out of an adventure story of the most lurid kind, and quite out of keeping with her character; but more and more, as the war dragged on, Edith Cavell found herself acting out of character: taking decisions and chances which were contrary to her upbringing and nature. Throughout those months of unreality she kept her eyes fixed on the one guiding star which had never ceased to shine over her life: to save and succor those in distress, whoever they were.

16

"Monsieur Baucq — may I talk to you for a few moments?"

"Mademoiselle Thuliez! But of course. Come inside." The young architect opened the door of his house more widely and held out his hand. Instinctively, Louise glanced up and down the street behind her before she stepped across the threshold. No one was about; so far, so good.

"But I am not Louise Thuliez at the moment, you know." She smiled. "I am Madame Lejeune. Louise Thuliez is too notorious a character with the Germans for her to be abroad in Brussels."

Philippe Baucq laughed. "I will remember — but what is it that Madame Lejeune wants with me?"

Louise immediately became serious. "The French Government needs more mechanics and metalworkers. You know we have sent some already. Now another group from the Maubeuge region is willing to go, if we can help them to cross the frontier into Holland. Will you take them? There are quite a lot — they will have to go in several groups."

"Of course."

"Then I think it would be wise if I had somewhere to stay which is close to your house. Can you recommend a boardinghouse where too many questions would not be asked about my comings and goings?"

Philippe Baucq thought for a moment. "I believe I know of such a place. I will make inquiries for you. Where are you staying at the moment?"

"At a hotel near the Gare du Midi."

"Why not come here, to my house, for tonight? Then tomorrow we can make other arrangements."

"That would be wonderful. Then we could talk . . . make our plans without too much coming and going. I have some people to see this evening but I could come back late — about half past ten?"

Monsieur Baucq nodded. He opened the front door again and a flood of July sunshine streamed down on them. Louise felt the warmth of it as she stepped out, and the strong, confident grip of Monsieur Baucq's hand in hers. She was smiling as she went up the street.

The sunshine had been gone for many hours when she returned later that night, but the warmth which had soaked into the walls of the houses bathed the air with a gentle, comforting glow. She thought of the many days she had spent in the Mormal Forest, her wet skirts whipping against her frozen legs, the damp squelching through the thin soles of her inadequate shoes. How much easier their dangerous work was when the weather gods smiled! From habit she moved without sound along the hard pavement, keeping automatically to the friendly shadows. There were few people about, and the street, after the lighted trolley car on which she had made part of the journey, seemed blacker than ever. But Louise was used to darkness and she walked swiftly, unerringly on her way.

The door of the Baucq's house was opened quickly to her knock. In the living room the scene was a cozy and reassuring one. Gathered round the table were Madame Baucq and her two little girls of eleven and fourteen, and two slightly older nieces. They were busy folding freshly printed copies of *La Libre Belgique,* ready for the next morning's delivery. They looked up and smiled at her as she entered the room.

"Now, that is enough for this evening," Madame Baucq remarked soon after Louise's arrival. "It is long past your bedtime, girls, so off you go." She turned to Louise with a smile. "And I'm sure you are ready for your bed too, Mademoiselle Thuliez. Come, I will show you to your room." She paused at the door. "Philippe, don't forget that the dog has not been out all evening, will you? He should have a little moment out of doors before you lock up."

Monsieur Baucq nodded, and Louise heard him go to the front door, the family dog frisking at his heels, as she walked up the stairs. Her mind, trained to note every unfamiliar sound, registered the click of the door latch, the sound of her host's footstep on the hard ground, and then . . .

The wild, hysterical barking of the dog and the brusque, guttural voices of invisible men sent her darting, with beating heart, into the shadows of the dimly lit landing. Instinct, sharpened by months of near escapes, told her that danger was in the air. She could almost smell it. Peering over the banister she saw, as if in a nightmare come true, a sea of field-gray uniforms.

One voice rose above the rest. "Where is the woman who came in here just now?"

One of the soldiers looked up, and for a fleeting moment their eyes met. The next instant, booted feet were pounding up the stairs. Louise turned and thrust open the door of the nearest room. It was a bathroom. With a convulsive movement she hurled her handbag behind the bath. Then a steely grip fastened on her wrist. With a savage push the soldier threw her against the wall and strode forward to where the shabby bag, with its revealing contents, lay half open on the floor.

17

FOR THREE DAYS after the arrest of Philippe Baucq and Louise Thuliez the nurses in the rue de la Culture walked on tiptoe, pausing to listen to the thud of their own hearts, starting at the rustle of each other's skirts. Sister Wilkins moved mechanically about her duties, eyes straying frequently to the windows, ears alert for the ominous peal of the front-door bell.

The Prince de Cröy, lines of strain around his tired eyes, called briefly and left grave-faced, his plea that Edith Cavell should attempt to escape quietly but firmly rejected.

"It would be useless," Edith told her second-in-command. "I am bound to be arrested at any moment now." She turned back to her desk. "You will be able to start moving into the new building early next week. I'm afraid it will be a long job. Tell José to be careful with the packing, so many things are irreplaceable now, and we only have the handcart for moving them."

Elisabeth Wilkins turned to the door, her lips trembling. She knew, none better, what the new hospital meant to her Matron; how she had fought for all it stood for, through eight long years. Fate could hardly have chosen a crueler moment to play its last, cruel trick. But she hid the tears which sprang to her eyes. Who was she to cry, when Matron, who was in much greater danger, remained so splendidly unperturbed? She tried to think of something cheerful — hopeful — to say, but the words stuck in her throat. Nor could she turn and look again into the clear gray eyes which were so full of knowledge and acceptance of what was to come.

All she could do to show her love and admiration was to carry out Matron's instructions. With a sigh, she opened the door and went in search of José. It was already early August. If they were to be thoroughly settled in the new building before the dark days came, she must lose no time. And at least the new preoccupations would keep her mind from darker thoughts.

Early August — a bitter time for the people of Belgium. For a whole year the gray uniforms of the invaders had stalked the city streets and struck an alien note in the one-time peaceful countryside. Daily their grip grew tighter, their punishments for disobedience harsher, their anger more sudden and violent. The first year of war had brought miseries and deprivations beyond anything the Belgians had dreamed of. What would the new year bring? Peace? Victory? Or more, and worse, misfortunes?

To Elisabeth Wilkins, opening to the morning light eyes which seemed filled with grit, there seemed to be only one answer to that question — an answer which filled her with dread. As she dressed, her fingers, cold in spite of the summer sun, fumbled over the fastenings of the starched

154

collar and belt of her uniform. Outside her door the familiar sounds of the hospital spoke of normality, but the significant date on the calendar taunted her from the wall: August 4th, 1915.

Later in the day, when she was halfway up the stairs to her afternoon conference in Matron's office she stopped dead, clinging to the handrail. Behind the closed door at the head of the staircase voices were raised in anger. There was a brief pause. She thought she caught the quiet tones of Nurse Cavell, but before she could be sure, the shouting had started again — ugly, staccato sounds like the crackle of gunfire. She leaned against the wall, crushing down her rising panic. There had been innumerable visits from the Secret Police, she told herself. They had never found anything. They would find nothing this time. All incriminating documents had long ago been destroyed. Since the Princess de Cröy's visit no fugitives had been housed in the clinic. She herself had guarded the door with vigilance, "heading off" stray callers to other, safer hide-outs, knowing that if they were once to get in contact with Nurse Cavell, nothing would stop her giving them sanctuary, however great the danger to herself.

But self-comforting arguments were of no avail. With the instinct of a forest animal when the hunt is up, she knew that this visit was different. The police were no longer searching for evidence. They had what they needed. Slowly she drew herself upright. She had heard that great disasters brought with them great strength with which to fight them. She prayed that this strength might be given to her now.

The door at the head of the stairs crashed open. A figure in the all-too-familiar field-gray appeared in the doorway, blocking out the light. "You." He pointed to her. "Come here, you."

With lifted head she climbed the last few stairs to the door of Nurse Cavell's office.

The rest of the day dragged. From behind the locked door of her sitting room Elisabeth heard the slam of drawers, the rattle of doorhandles, guttural commands and responses, the tramp of booted feet. The hands seemed glued to the face of the clock and the sun to have stopped in the sky. When she closed her eyes the white, calm face of Miss Cavell — expressionless after one fleeting glance of encouragement and affection — seemed printed on the inside of her eyelids. When she opened them the familiar objects of her sitting room mocked her with their very ordinariness in a situation so full of melodrama.

When at last the key grated in the lock she seemed too drained of emotion to feel anything but relief. Anything was better than waiting . . . wondering . . .

"Bring what you need for one night, and come quickly."

"Where . . ." Elisabeth began, then she bit back the question. Useless — and unnecessary — to ask. It could only be to Police Headquarters for another, interminable interrogation. With cold but steady hands she packed the small case, hating to expose her shabby intimate possessions to the insolent stare of the waiting soldier. Then, with head held proudly high, she swept past him through the door.

Edith Cavell was already waiting by the front door, her

own small case in her hand. Almost imperceptibly she shook her head as Elisabeth opened her mouth to speak, then she turned and walked quietly into the open air. A big gray car, heavily guarded, was waiting for them in the street. Silently they climbed into it. Out of the corner of her eye Elisabeth could see the still, pale face of her companion who sat like a statue, glancing neither to right nor to left. It was as if she were guarding the reserves of strength which Elisabeth herself had prayed for earlier in the day.

Elisabeth drew comfort from her nearness. She seemed to radiate courage and tranquility; to reduce any situation to an everyday level. The melodrama of the day, with its locked doors, Secret Police, guarded motors, seemed suddenly to become something almost matter-of-fact. What had happened, after all? They had, contrary to the invaders' laws, hidden a number of soldiers and "wanted" civilians and helped them to achieve freedom. Their activities had been discovered. They were about to be questioned. The worst that could come out of it was a period of imprisonment. After the agonizing suspense of the last few months, even that did not frighten Elisabeth as once it might have done.

By the time the motor slowed down and stopped outside the Police Headquarters confidence was beginning to flow back into her. She had only to think carefully before she spoke; deny anything which might incriminate herself or her colleagues and even now she might escape their clutches.

"In here." With a jerk of his head the soldier indicated

the door of a room. Elisabeth stepped forward. On the point of entering she paused and turned, but already Edith Cavell was being led away down the corridor. She looked pitifully small and slight between the two burly figures in field-gray, but even from the back there was something . . . something unshakable, and unbreakable, about her.

As she disappeared round a corner at the end of the corridor, Elisabeth turned back to the bare little room and entered it. She did not feel quite as confident as she had a moment or so ago, but the hard core of strength was still there. She was not going to give up yet.

The shadows were long in the streets when, at last, she stepped out through the door of the Police Headquarters again. The air tasted stale and overused; it smelled of stone and dust and hot metal and horses, but she drew it gratefully into her lungs in big gulps. Back there in the Police Headquarters, even to breathe freely had seemed reckless.

Her head ached, and every nerve in her body felt tired with the effort of watchfulness, but her brain refused to slow down. Who were the men they had sheltered? How many were there? Who had guided them to the frontier? How had they crossed it — and where? Were they English? Belgian? French? Who had brought them to the clinic? The questions beat against her like hammers. They seemed to pursue her as she sped through the quiet streets; to sigh among the branches of the trees and echo in the sound of her own footsteps. As she turned into the rue de la Culture her steps quickened. Had Matron returned already? Or . . . She pushed the thought from her mind as she fumbled for her key. She must not lose heart. If Matron had not returned she would have to assume responsibility for the clinic, for the nurses, for the complicated removal operations to the new building. She would need every ounce of composure and strength. And in her heart she already knew that that strength would be needed.

As she pushed open the door that belief became a certainty. Inside, the nurses stood about in subdued groups, or went about their duties with red, swollen eyes. Matron might be — was — stern and uncompromising where duty was concerned, but there was not one nurse who did not remember some unobtrusive kindness; a gentle word of understanding when her personal world had been grim and overshadowed by sorrow or loss. Though she rarely spoke unnecessarily, was often missing from the clinic on her many visits to other hospitals, her personality seemed to dominate the very walls and corridors about which she had moved with quiet efficiency. Her invisible presence was everywhere, and yet there was an aching emptiness throughout the whole building.

The shadows lengthened, and night came. Slowly, one by one, the nurses went to their beds, to lie awake, or to sleep an unrefreshing sleep of exhaustion. At her window, Elisabeth Wilkins kept a self-imposed vigil until reluctantly she was forced to admit to herself that the austere rooms which had sheltered her Matron for so long would remain empty that night, and probably for many nights to come. Reluctantly she undressed and climbed into bed. The work of the clinic must go on. It would be the first thought, the first wish, of its Matron; and if she were to play her part, rest and sleep were of first importance.

As she put out her hand to extinguish the light, the calendar which had taunted her that morning jeered at her anew: August 4th — the anniversary of the outbreak of war: a date none of them would ever forget. Was it, now, to have an even more horrifying meaning?

18

THE FORTRESSLIKE prison of St. Gilles stood on the outskirts of Brussels. No city sounds penetrated its high walls, and once the vast, heavy door had clanged to behind the prisoners they were as cut off from their former world as if they had been spirited away to another planet.

In her tiny cell, late on the night of her arrest, Edith Cavell was alone, physically as well as spiritually, for the first time for many years. No one would come tapping on her door with a question, a responsibility to be shifted onto stronger shoulders, a problem to be solved. There had been, and would be, many questions of a different kind, but for the moment at least no one would turn to her for help. It was strangely restful, after so many years of ceaseless activity. She felt almost happy.

A faint gleam of moonlight crept through the high window to lay a cold finger on the spartan furnishings: a folding bed, a wooden stool, a tiny corner cupboard and a pitcher of water. If she turned her head a little she could see the spyhole in the door where every now and again the beam of a torch flashed as the jailers did their rounds.

The bleakness of her surroundings caused her no distress. For choice she had always lived simply and now she was almost unaware of the starkness of the room in which she lay. She was only aware that for once she had time to think: of what she had done, of what had happened to her, of what was to come. She searched her conscience, and found it clear. If she were to live this year over again, she would do exactly the same again. That she might have been instrumental in saving lives she was grateful. If it meant the sacrifice of her own liberty, she had no regrets. She held fast to her beliefs, and they gave her strength and inner peace. When at last she slept, the lines smoothed out from her face and there was, for a few hours, a look about her of the young Edith who had laughed and played in the fields and lanes of Swardeston, forty years before.

The mood of detachment did not persist beyond the next day. She knew that on the other side of the city her nurses would be waiting, wondering — questioning each other in low tones. She could not leave them in suspense. Worse still — lovely Grace Jemmett, who had clung so closely to her for many years now, would be anchorless in a frightening world. She had been allowed to keep her pen and some writing paper, and towards the end of her first full day in prison she sat down to write the words of love and comfort which she knew would be needed so badly:

> My dearest Gracie,
>
> I do hope you are not worrying about me — tell everyone that I am quite all right here — I suppose from what I hear that I shall be questioned one of these days, and when they have all they desire I

shall know what they mean to do with me. We are numerous here and there is no chance of being lonely. We can buy food at the canteen, but I should be glad to have one of our red blankets, a serviette, cup, fork and spoon and plate — not the best ones — also one or two towels and my toothbrush, a tea cloth and pair of cuffs. In a day or two some clean linen. I'm afraid you will not be able to come and see me at present but you can write, only your letters will be read. Is Sister Wilkins free? I have been thinking of her ever since last night. Tell them to go on with the move as before. If Sister is there she will know how to arrange everything.

Is Jackie sad? Tell him I will be back soon.

The day is rather long. Can you send me a book and a little embroidery, also some nail scissors — only a *very few* things as I have no place to put them . . . Remember me to all the Sisters, nurses and household.

There is a small child of three or four here with her mother; she looks pale and pinched for want of air, though she is allowed out a little every day.

I will write again when there is anything to tell. Don't, don't worry. We must hope for the best. Tell them all to go on as usual . . .

It was so like her, even at such a moment, to notice and be concerned about a child's pallor, a fretting dog; to remember and note that a prison cell was no fit place for the *best* china . . . not to expect others to think for her, but to think for herself, and for them too.

163

Unshakable, unbreakable, Sister Wilkins had thought of her as she walked away down the corridor of the Police Headquarters. And the next few weeks were to prove it beyond all doubt. And still she continued to think of others. She wrote another, longer, letter to her nurses:

St. Gilles Prison,
14th September 1915

My dear Nurses,

Your delightful letter gave me great pleasure, and your lovely flowers have made my cell gay — the roses are still fresh, but the chrysanthemums did not like prison any more than I do — hence they did not live very long.

I am happy to know that you are working well, that you are devoted to your patients and that you are happy in your services. It is necessary that you should study well, for some of you must shortly sit for your examinations and I want you very much to succeed. The year's course will commence shortly, try to profit from it, and be punctual at lectures so that your professor need not be kept waiting.

In everything one can learn new lessons of life, and if you were in my place you would realise how precious liberty is, and would certainly undertake never to abuse it.

To be a good nurse one must have lots of patience — here one learns to have that quality, I assure you.

It appears that the new School is advancing — I

164

hope to see it again one of these days, as well as all
of you.

Au revoir. Be really good.
Your devoted Matron,
E. CAVELL

Day followed dragging day. The heat went out of the
sun, and the deep blue of the sky thinned to an autumn
pastel. She read, did a little embroidery, wrote letters to
her family and friends and thought a great deal about the
past, and the future. There was little doubt in her mind
that it would be many years, now, before she saw the new
Ecole belge d'Infirmières diplômées on which she had
lavished so much love and thought; but she drew comfort
from the knowledge that, wherever she was, and whatever
happened to her, her work would go on. The Nursing
Service was strong enough now to stand on its own feet.
The standards she had set were firmly implanted. Already
"her" nurses were carrying her teaching into hospitals all
over Belgium. She was content. There was much more
she would have wished to do, but if she accomplished no
more, then she was humbly grateful for the opportunities
which had been offered to her already.

Gradually, the small world of the prison closed about
her. The monotonous routine of the day was broken only
by brief periods of exercise in the tiny triangles of garden,
separated from each other by high stone walls and watched
over by the officer of the guard; and the brief — all too
brief and all too rare — visits by friends from outside,
equally heavily guarded so that no conversation except the

165

most impersonal was possible. Twice Sister Wilkins was allowed to see her. They spoke of the move to the new building, of the routine of the clinic, of the nurses and patients, and domestic trivialities. Only their eyes could convey the messages that really mattered, and at the end of each visit, Sister Wilkins left with a heavy heart.

At night, when darkness laid its softening mantle over the bleak, forbidding building, ears became sharpened to the sounds which struck fresh hopelessness into the listeners in the cells: the blare of motor horns as the big German army cars arrived in the prison yard, bringing new victims; the rattle of doors opening, and the doom-filled clang as they crashed to behind them. The sharp ring of orders along the corridors and footsteps on the hard floors, and then the dying fall of anguished sobbing from the newly filled cells.

Such sounds underlined Edith's growing conviction that her own liberty was more or less permanently at an end — a conviction which increased with each successive cross-examination by the German Police. It was obvious that they already knew so much. On the night of Philippe Baucq's arrest hundreds of copies of *La Libre Belgique* had been found in the garden of his house — hastily thrown there by his wife and daughters when the house was invaded by soldiers. There had been other documents too: one mentioning her name. Even among her own papers they had found one letter from England which she had neglected to destroy, and Louise Thuliez's handbag had yielded a treasure-trove of incriminating evidence. Of what use was it to argue such facts?

Besides, they told her, the other prisoners had confessed to the part they, and she, had played in the organization of mass escapes.

"We know this has been going on since last November. We know that you have given these men shelter, food and money. We know that, apart from soldiers, you have helped able-bodied men from France and Belgium to reach enemy territory, where they have joined the fight against Germany." They spoke with the confidence that comes of absolute knowledge; and Edith agreed that all they said was true. She had done what they said; it seemed pointless to add denial and lies to the growing horror that war had brought into her life.

Honest and straightforward as she was, it did not occur to her that many of the statements they made were based on inspired guesses, and fragments of evidence; or that the same sort of trickery had been used on other prisoners to extract information, and that such fragments, pieced together, were weaving a noose for all of them.

"Do you think these men were grateful for what you did?" There was a sneer in the voice of her inquisitor. "Do you think for one moment they gave another thought to the woman who risked her life for them?"

"I know they were grateful," Edith replied, stung by the suggestion.

"How?" There was barely concealed eagerness in the man's voice.

"They wrote and told me that they had arrived safely at their destination, and thanked me for the help I had given them."

167

A sigh went through the empty room; a sigh of mingled triumph and incredulity. Could any woman be so foolish as to knock the nails into her own coffin with such a confession? Only a very simple one, their contemptuous glances seemed to say. But in that respect Edith Cavell was very simple. She did not understand the tortuous twists and turns of the Prussian mind. Even after the experiences of the past year, truth and right were still, to her, immovable, intransmutable and eternal. If she broke the laws of the Germans, they might punish her body. If she broke her own laws, and those of God, she would destroy her soul.

Being the person she was, she had no defense against the agile and unscrupulous minds of the German Police, and she was not even allowed, by their law, to meet the defense counsel who was to fight her case at the court-martial that was being prepared. All the carefully gathered "facts" that were being built into a damning case against her were secreted from him until the moment of revelation in court. The Germans held all the cards, and they were playing to win.

The day of the trial dawned at last. For the first time for many years Edith Cavell laid aside her nurse's uniform. For her it was a symbol of a high and meritorious calling. She would not dishonor it by exposing it to the mocking gaze of a German military court. When she dressed, with all her usual neatness and care, it was in a plain blue coat and hat; and when, with thirty-four other "prisoners at the bar," she stepped into the awe-inspiring Senate Chamber to stand trial for her life, she appeared no more than an

168

"ordinary little woman," divested of authority and the outward trappings which might, with the German love of uniform, have instilled in the judges a modicum of respect.

She was not the only one to be diminished in status by the circumstances of the court-martial. All the prisoners looked shabby and pathetic against the vast splendor of the hall in which they were to be tried. Huge murals representing important events in Belgian history loomed over them; the red-velvet-covered chairs of the Belgian Senators threw into mocking relief their prison pallor and threadbare garments. In appearance there was nothing about them to excite respect in the minds of the five German officers who sat in judgment over them — and they certainly received none.

Edith Cavell was the first to be cross-questioned. She spoke quietly, without a tremor. She had, she said, simply done what she thought was her duty in saving the lives of men whom she knew were in danger of death. That was all. It was enough, in the eyes of the Germans, to brand her as a criminal. Louise Thuliez followed her before the judges, and then Philippe Baucq.

At noon enormous pots of steaming, savory-smelling soup were brought into court for the soldiers left in charge of the prisoners during the lunch recess. Nothing whatever was brought for the prisoners themselves who sat, swallowing convulsively and trying to keep their eyes from the steaming bowls which tantalized their gastric juices into working overtime. Just a few of the prisoners had, with surprising forethought, brought a meager supply of food to the court with them, and they shared it with the

169

others. It was little enough, but sufficient to parch their throats. One or two of the soldiers, moved by compassion, offered them water in the glasses they themselves had used but, thirsty as they were, the prisoners could not bring themselves to share the glasses used by their jailers. Cupping their palms, they poured the water into the hollow and sucked it up like thirsty children picnicking by a country stream.

Under cover of the mealtime relaxation, Louise managed to snatch a few words with Edith, who sat just in front of her. How were things going, did she think?

Edith half turned in her seat. "I think Baucq, Capiau, you and I stand a bad chance," she whispered softly. "But what does it matter — so long as we are not shot?"

At two o'clock the lawyers and judges returned and the trial went on. Throughout the long afternoon it dragged, the judges frequently whispering together over the green-covered *Manual of the German Military Code.* At seven o'clock it was adjourned until the next day and the prisoners taken back to St. Gilles, to spend another night of tense anxiety and, when they slept, nightmare dreams.

The second day was, for the prisoners, much like the first. There were speeches and counterspeeches, pleas and counterpleas — incomprehensible to most of them until they were translated into French. Sitting there either stiff with dread or limp with apathy, they felt that the words had little bearing on what would eventually happen. The whole trial had taken on, for them, the air of a vast, hypocritical charade.

After each speech by the Defense, the prisoner defended

was given the chance to speak for himself. When Edith's turn came she moved with dignity in front of the Judge's bench, head high and back straight.

"When I first turned my attention to this work . . ." she began in a small, clear voice.

"Yes, yes . . . you've told us all that before. Go back to your place," interrupted the Military Prosecutor testily.

For a second, unable to believe that she was not to be given the chance to speak after all, Edith stood as still as a statue. Then, as the Military Prosecutor made another, more violent gesture of impatience, she turned and walked slowly back to her seat, her eyes sparkling with tears. The other prisoners glanced at one another with sinking hearts. This seemed to bode no good for any of them.

But it was not until the Military Prosecutor came to ask for the sentences that they fully realized the gravity of their situation. Up to the last moment they clung to the hope that since their motives had been patriotic, their sentences would be light. Only as the interpreter, in a voice almost devoid of expression, translated the Prosecutor's demands, did a ripple of unbelieving horror sweep over the hall. For many of those only lightly involved in the organization the demand was for a sentence of many years' hard labor. But for the leaders: Cavell, Thuliez, Baucq, Severin, Belleville, Bodart, Libiez and Capiau, the Prosecutor would be satisfied by nothing but death.

19

EDITH's friends had not been idle during her months in prison. The American Legation in Brussels had authority to handle the affairs of English people still resident there, and their legal adviser, Maître de Leval, pestered the German authorities for information . . . for permission to see Nurse Cavell . . . for permission to arrange for her defense. In vain. The head of the Legation himself wrote persistent letters, sent telegrams, and telephoned for news of the trial . . . In vain. A shroud of impenetrable secrecy descended over the prison and courtroom. "There is no news yet"; "judgment had not yet been pronounced"; "the American Legation would be informed in due course." Requests, demands, pleas, all were met by the same blank wall of evasion.

Late on the afternoon of October 11th — two days after the end of the trial — a white-faced nurse burst unceremoniously into Sister Wilkins's sitting room in the rue de la Culture.

"Sister — my father has just been here. He's heard rumors . . . rumors . . ." She stopped, her mouth trembling, then she went on in a whisper. "He's heard that Matron has been — sentenced to death. She's to be shot, early tomorrow morning."

Sister Wilkins stared at her for a moment in horrified disbelief. Then at last: "What exactly did he hear, and where did he hear it," she asked in a voice curiously unlike her own.

"His office window overlooks the courthouse. He heard some German officers talking. Sister — what can we *do?*"

After her moment of shock, feeling and a frantic desire to take action seized Sister Wilkins. She snatched her cape from the hook on the back of the door and flung it round her shoulders. "Perhaps nothing. But I'm going to try . . . at least to find out if it's true."

Halfway down the stairs she met Nurse Smith, one of the Private Staff nurses, whose eyes widened with alarm at the sight of Elisabeth's distraught face. "Sister — what on earth's happened? Where are you going?"

It needed only a few words to explain the whole appalling situation. "Come with me to the prison," Sister Wilkins begged. "We *must* find out if it's true."

Without a word, Nurse Smith turned and ran to her room. She paused only to grab her coat and throw it over her uniform. A moment later they were hurrying down the street.

At the prison gate they paused simultaneously, and turned to look at each other. Which was worse, their eyes asked — this terrible doubt, or to know for certain that the hideous rumor was true?

Sister Wilkins raised her hand and touched the bell. Its

peal seemed to echo despairingly along the corridors of the vast, frowning building.

Even as they stood before the great gate, guards were unlocking the cell doors inside. Edith Cavell looked up from the table where she was reading, at the inscrutable face of the man standing before her.

"Get ready to come and receive your sentence," he said briefly.

She rose and smoothed the dark stuff of her dress with trembling hands, but her eyes were steady as she walked past him into the corridor. In the central hall of the prison her fellow prisoners were waiting, white-faced and subdued. In the silence which followed their assembling they heard the clank of footsteps. The German chaplain, followed by two high-ranking officers and the Military Prosecutor, entered the hall. His eyes swept compassionately across the faces of the prisoners, then he bowed his head.

Into the electric silence which followed their arrival the harsh voice of the Military Prosecutor dropped the fatal words. Five times the German *Todesstrafe* splintered the tense atmosphere, following the names of Philippe Baucq, Louise Thuliez, Edith Cavell, Louis Severin and Jeanne de Belleville. The French translation which followed was superfluous; all the prisoners had read the sign of death in the faces of the men who confronted them.

Louise Thuliez glanced at her fellow victims. Edith Cavell stood as if turned to stone, her face livid with shock as the import of the sentence penetrated her mind.

The Prosecutor's voice droned on, but even those to whom long and arduous prison sentences were being meted

174

out hardly heeded his words. Death . . . death . . . the word rang in their ears, excluding everything that followed.

The Prosecutor finished his proclamation, swung round on his heel and left the hall. Like sleepwalkers the prisoners turned in obedience to the gestures of the guards and began to file silently back towards their cells, past the still figure of the German pastor who had remained motionless, his head still bent in sorrow.

The Countess de Belleville stretched out a hand tentatively towards him. "Is there nothing — nothing more we can do?" she asked in a low voice.

Before he could answer, one of the two officers stepped forward. "You may write an appeal for mercy direct to the Governor General," he told her quietly. "There is nothing more to be done here."

Louise turned her head. Beside her, Edith Cavell was standing perfectly still. "Is that what you will do?" she whispered.

Edith shook her head. "No. For me it would be useless. I am English," she answered simply. "And the Germans cannot forgive the English for standing in their way." The second officer stepped forward and touched her arm. Without a further word or look she followed him out of the hall.

20

OUTSIDE the prison it had begun to rain. Drops of water frosted Elisabeth Wilkins's hair and the shoulders of her cloak as she leaned forward to talk to the warder who had opened the gate to her ring.

"But surely you can tell me something," she persisted.

"Mademoiselle, I have already told you all I know. Only a short time ago the prisoners were paraded in the central hall, to hear the verdict on their cases. Naturally I do not know what the verdict is." Looking at her distraught face he was moved by sympathy. "But Maître de Leval, the lawyer, is sure to have been told. Why do you not go to see him? I would tell you if I could, but truly, I know nothing . . ." He spread his hands in a gesture of helplessness.

Elisabeth felt a fleeting touch on her arm. She turned. Nurse Smith shook her head slightly. "We are getting nowhere here," she said. "Let's do as he suggests."

Elisabeth sighed, reluctantly. Even though she knew, in her heart, that she could do no good there, she was loath to leave the prison. She looked up at the dumb, towering walls. Somewhere behind them Matron was perhaps even now listening to the words which were cutting her off from everything she held dear — from life itself. She shivered, then obedient to the gentle tug of Nurse Smith's hand, she turned from the prison gate.

"Of course you're right," she said dully.

The warder stood for a moment in the doorway, watching the two small, disconsolate figures hurry away into the gathering darkness, then the door of the prison shut with a final, significant thud.

The two girls hurried along, each lost in her own unhappy thoughts, oblivious of the rain which had turned from a drizzle to a soaking downpour. At the door of Maître de Leval's house they waited in silence for an answer to their ring, almost beyond hope now, yet unable to give up their quest. "While there's life, there's hope . . . While there's life, there's hope . . ." The jingle repeated itself interminably in Elisabeth's head until the words themselves ceased to have meaning and only the rhythm of the trite little saying remained — something for her grief-stricken mind to cling to, and to prevent other, more horrifying thoughts from driving her into the darkness.

Maître de Leval listened to their breathless, almost incoherent story in grim silence. He knew nothing of this, he assured them. There had been no telephone call, no message. Perhaps the Embassy . . . ? He snatched up a coat and opened the door. They must come with him — quickly. There was no time to be lost. The wet and windy street claimed them once more. Numbed as she was by grief, Elisabeth no longer felt the lash of rain in her face, or the creeping discomfort of wet shoes. "While there's life . . ." her tired brain insisted. She glanced up at the set face of the man hurrying along at her side, and tried hard to hope.

In the warm, bright room at the Embassy into which they were shown, she waited in silence with Nurse Smith, while Maître de Leval went to consult the American Minister, who was ill in bed. The slow, measured tick of the clock was all that broke the silence. A small, bright fire burned in the grate — an almost unheard-of luxury after a year of war. The girls stretched their stiff fingers gratefully in front of the flames. At last the door opened, and Maître de Leval returned.

"I am to present a Petition for Mercy to the Governor General," he told them hurriedly. "Wait here — I will bring news just as soon as I can. Good news, I hope." He tried to smile hopefully, but his eyes did not echo the curve of his mouth.

He had only been gone a few moments when the door reopened. Elisabeth half rose from her seat. Mr. Gahan, the pastor of the English church in Brussels, was standing in the doorway, a look of bewilderment on his face, a crumpled piece of paper in his hand. He held it out to Elisabeth. "Someone brought this from St. Gilles," he said. "I'm afraid it might mean . . ."

Slowly Elisabeth unfolded the paper. Hurriedly scrawled in pencil across it were the melodramatic words: "Come at once — someone is about to die."

"You'll go to her?" she asked.

The pastor nodded. "Of course. At once. My wife

would like to wait here with you until I return." He turned and drew forward a sad-faced woman whose eyes filled with tears at the sight of Elisabeth's uniform. At that moment the front-door bell rang again. There was a subdued murmur of voices and again the door opened. A little cluster of wide-eyed nurses stood on the threshold.

"Oh, Sister what . . . what's going to happen?" The youngest of them flung herself impulsively into Elisabeth's arms. "They say that Matron . . . that Matron . . ." She burst into tears.

"Now Nurse, crying won't help anyone, least of all Matron. Pull yourself together." Elisabeth disengaged herself gently and patted the girl's hand. Her own tears were scarcely dry on her cheeks, but she knew that for the moment at least they were a luxury she could not afford. The mantle of responsibility that Miss Cavell had carried so long was heavy on her shoulders, but at least it was one burden she could bear for her. She put her arm round the little nurse's shoulders and drew her into a chair. "Try not to cry, Nurse," she said. "Everything possible is being done for Matron. We must be patient, now — and wait."

Everything possible *was* being done. Maître de Leval had hurried off into the wet darkness in search of Hugh Gibson, Secretary to the American Legation, and the Marquis de Lillalobar, the distinguished Spanish Ambassador, to support his urgent plea for mercy; and Mr. Gahan, his heart heavy with sorrow and anxiety, was making his way to St. Gilles. There was nothing more the little group of nurses could do but wait . . . and wait . . . and wait. The fire flapped small, brave banners in the grate; the

179

clock ticked remorselessly on and they sat, huddled in the formal Embassy chairs, their dull eyes staring ahead of them.

On the far side of the city, keys were grating in the locks and footsteps echoed hollowly along corridors as the guards led Mr. Gahan through the maze of passages in the vast, gloomy prison. Even the blank-faced doors of the cells seemed to be listening as he passed them and the chill in the air was surely compounded of more than just the autumn winds and rain?

The guard halted and slipped a key into one door which showed no outward sign of difference from those which flanked it. It creaked open and Mr. Gahan moved into the narrow cell.

He was shocked by the changed appearance of the slight figure who rose from the bed as he entered. Nurse Cavell had always seemed to him slender and delicately proportioned, but there had been an underlying toughness and energy about her which spoke of reserves of youthful power. Now, after ten weeks of imprisonment, every sign of youth had vanished. The lamplight touched her silvery hair and the frail, prominent bones of her face. The skin, stretched across it, looked almost transparent and her gray eyes large and shadowed under their level brows.

She held out her hand. "It is good of you to come," she said quietly. As she smiled into his face he had the fleeting impression that it was to him that comfort was being given. And her first words strengthened his conviction.

"I have no fear nor shrinking," she assured him. "I have seen death so often it is not strange or fearful to me." She

180

sat down on the edge of her narrow prison bed and gestured to the hard, upright chair which stood close by. Mr. Gahan sat down on it. The first moments of tension had slipped away. The softly lit cell had now a sense of intimacy and withdrawal from the world. He no longer felt burdened by the Last Rites he had come to administer. Tranquillity and resignation had made his task a bearable, even an exalting one.

"I thank God for this ten weeks' quiet before the end," Edith went on. "Life has always been hurried and full of difficulty. This time of rest has been a great mercy. Everyone here has been very kind." She looked down at her hands, lying folded in her lap, and then up again, straight into Mr. Gahan's face. Clearly and steadily, as if this were a message she would give to the world, she added: "This I would say — standing as I do in view of God and Eternity: I realize that patriotism is not enough. I must have no hatred or bitterness towards anyone."

There was silence for a moment. Then Mr. Gahan rose to his feet and began to prepare the ceremony of Holy Communion. At the end of the little service — as the silence began to close in on them once again — he began quietly to repeat the words of the hymn:

Abide with me; fast falls the eventide;
The darkness deepens; Lord, with me abide.
When other helpers fail, and comforts flee,
Help of the helpless, O abide with me.

Swift to its close ebbs out life's little day;
Earth's joys grow dim, its glories pass away.

Change and decay in all around I see;
O Thou who changest not, abide with me.

As the solemn words fell on the still night air Edith first listened, kneeling in silence, and then, as the hymn drew to a close, she softly joined in:

Hold Thou Thy cross before my closing eyes;
Shine through the gloom and point me to the skies;
Heaven's morning breaks, and earth's vain shadows flee;
In life, in death, O Lord, abide with me.

She was smiling as she rose from her knees, and her eyes were serene. They sat down together again and talked of her family, and the nurses she was leaving behind to carry on with the work she had so arduously begun. She gave Mr. Gahan messages for her mother and sisters, her cousin Eddy and others whom she loved.

At last the time for parting came. Once more the thin, delicate hand slipped into Mr. Gahan's, and he felt the firm clasp of her fingers.

"Goodbye," he said gently.

She smiled, and almost imperceptibly shook her head. "We shall meet again," she replied.

21

NINE O'CLOCK . . . Ten o'clock . . . Eleven o'clock
. . . Midnight! Elisabeth's eyes felt like hot coals. She
blinked and rubbed them wearily. Surely there must be
news soon? Every dragging minute seemed like an eternity. Maddeningly the clock ticked on its even, unhurried
way. "While there's life . . . while — there's — life
. . ." it muttered. Then, with a subtle change of rhythm:
"No — good . . . no — good . . . no — good . . ." The
words danced in her aching head interminably. Nervously
she got to her feet and crossed to the window. A dozen
pairs of eyes followed her anxiously. She went back to her
chair. A moment later there was the sound of footsteps;
a door opened; voices . . . The nurses got to their feet
and drew instinctively close to each other in a protective
group. A hand stole into Elisabeth's and she squeezed it
comfortingly.

The door of the room opened. Maître de Leval, looking
white and drawn, entered, followed by a tall dark-haired
young man on whose face was a mixture of anger, frustra-

tion and pity. There was no need for them to speak. One of the nurses behind Elisabeth began to sob convulsively.

"It's no use," Hugh Gibson, the dark young man, said bitterly. "We've tried every argument . . . They won't even accept the formal plea for mercy. At first they wouldn't even admit that the execution was timed for tomorrow morning." His face darkened at some memory, then his eyes swept round the stricken little group. "We did our best," he said, almost defensively.

"Of course." Elisabeth spoke quickly, compassionately. The night had been a nightmare for her and her fellow nurses. How much worse it must have been for these two who had fought so hard, and been forced to admit bitter defeat. "We must go." She took a step forward. "Thank you for all you have done."

Silently the two men stepped back, and the little procession of nurses trailed out of the room. Outside it was still raining, steadily and unemphatically. The pavements glistened and windows glinted grayly against the damp-darkened stone and brick. Suddenly Elisabeth felt overwhelmingly, desperately tired. But sleep refused to come when — half an hour later — she reached the quiet seclusion of her room in the new clinic. Too many memories thronged the corridors of her mind; too many doubts and regrets propped up her eyelids and tormented her active brain. Was there anything — *anything* more any of them could have done? But she knew in her heart that nobody, and nothing, could have deflected Edith Cavell from the path she had chosen, once she had chosen it; and that

184

having chosen it, there could have been no other possible outcome.

Somewhere outside in the town a clock struck three. Shivering, she sat up. Through the crack under her door she could see a light shining. Footsteps moved stealthily along the corridor. Getting out of bed she went to the door. Nurse Smith, drawn-faced, wrapped in her dressing gown, was standing outside.

"I can't sleep," she pleaded.

"Neither can I. I'm going to dress and go out for a walk. Will you come?" Sister Wilkins said with sudden decision. Nurse Smith nodded.

"Perhaps if we went back to the prison . . . ?"

Sister Wilkins winced. "There's nothing we can do."

"I know. But . . ." Nurse Smith turned and walked back to her room, her head bent.

Ten minutes later the two, fully dressed, walked quietly down the corridor. Just as they were about to go down the stairs, several of the other nurses appeared in their door-ways. "Please — could we come too?" There was no need to ask, or explain, the destination. Sister Wilkins nodded listlessly. Rules and regulations had no meaning that night.

It had stopped raining, but a cool wind whipped their skirts about their ankles. Somewhere in the sky was a hint of daylight to come, but the thought gave them no comfort. It was to be a day they would never forget, and never remember without sadness: October 12th, 1915.

The great, forbidding bulk of the prison loomed up in

185

front of them. Pricks of light dotted its blank, unfriendly face. Beneath its walls the nurses felt dwarfed and utterly ineffectual. They huddled together for warmth, and to share their dwindling stock of courage and hope, trying to tell themselves that even at this late hour, a miracle might happen.

But there were few miracles in Brussels in October 1915, and this one was not to be. With the first streaks of dawn lightening the sky the vast gates of the prison swung open. Two big gray cars swept out — picking up speed rapidly. Through the blur of her tears Elisabeth caught one quick glimpse of a familiar white face in the leading car. Then it was gone. The arm she had half raised in greeting and salute fell to her side. The second car swept past. Was it Philippe Baucq, sitting there between the two blank-faced guards?

She closed her burning eyes as the two cars turned a corner, heading for the *Tir National* — the Belgian National Shooting Range. The big prison gates swung to. The sound of noisy engines died away in the distance. When she opened her eyes again, the sky above the prison was turning pink.

Inside the big gray car Edith Cavell sat erect and proud, looking for the last time on the city she had loved and served for so many years — smelling the country freshness of the rain-washed air. Her quick ear caught the sleepy twitter of a wakening bird. A new day was beginning . . . Strange to think that she would not see darkness fall when it ended.

186

The car stopped. An officer rapped out an order. With unhurried dignity she stepped out. Then, without a backward glance, and with all the steadfast courage she had brought to life, she went to her death.

Epilogue

THE EXECUTION of Edith Cavell shocked the whole world. That a woman — and a nurse — should have suffered such a fate seemed impossibly brutal at that time. Thirty years later, unfortunately, it had come to be accepted as a "natural" hazard of war, but in 1915 every civilized nation rose in horrified anger to condemn the German action. Recruiting in England rose to an unprecedented level. America was roused to new and greater indignation and resentment, and though it was to be two years before she actually took part in the fighting, it is probably no exaggeration to suggest that Edith Cavell's death, and the sinking of the *Lusitania* (in which Marie Depage lost her life), were two of the factors which governed her decision to participate in the war, and which led to the eventual turning of the tide against Germany.

Of all those who took part in the underground work of aiding fugitives, only Edith Cavell and Philippe Baucq were actually executed. Prince Reginald de Cröy escaped, by a hairbreadth, into Holland; the rest of those condemned to death had their sentences mitigated (after intervention by many people in high places) to hard labor, and at the end of the war received their freedom. Some may even still be alive.

But, although she is, today, looked upon as a great patriot, and an instrument of victory, Edith herself would probably have taken little pride in such a reputation. Nationalism was as foreign to her nature as the violence by which she died. She loved her homeland, as she loved Belgium, but did she not herself say: "Patriotism is not enough"? For her, people might differ in language, religion and customs, but to her they were all people, who needed the loving care and skilled attention which as a nurse she was able and trained to give them. "I must have no hatred or bitterness towards anyone," she had added. For her, the enemy was War itself, rather than the people who fought it.

Among her last thoughts were some for "her" nurses, and among her last letters was a message for them; expressing her hopes for the future in which she would not be able to share, and her memories of the difficult days they had shared:

My dear Nurses,

This is a sad moment for me, as I write to say goodbye. It reminds me that on the 17th September I had been running the school for eight years.

I was so happy to be called to help in the organisation of the work which our Committee had just founded. On the 1st October 1907 there were only four young pupils, whereas now you are many — fifty to sixty in all, I believe, including those who have gained their certificates and are about to leave the school.

I have often told you about those early days and the difficulties we met with, even down to the choice of words for your on-duty hours and your off-duty hours.

For Belgium, everything about the profession was new. Gradually one service after the other was set up; nurses for private needs, school nurses, the St Gilles hospital. We have staffed Dr Depage's Institute, the sanatorium at Buysingen, Dr Mayer's Clinic, and now many are called (as perhaps you will be later) to tend the brave men wounded in war. If our work has diminished during this last year, it is because of the sad time we are passing through; when better days come our work will grow again and recover all its power to do good.

If I have spoken to you of the past, this is because it is a good thing sometimes to stop and look back along the path we have travelled, to take stock of our progress and the mistakes we have made. You will have more patients in your fine house, and you will have everything necessary for their comfort and your own.

To my sorrow I have not always been able to talk to you each privately. You know that I had my share of burdens. But I hope that you will not forget our evening chats.

I told you that devotion would bring you true happiness and the thought that, before God and in your own eyes, you have done your duty well and with a good heart, will sustain you in trouble and

190

face to face with death. There are two or three of
you who will recall the little talks we had together.
Do not forget them. As I had already gone so far
along life's road, I was perhaps able to see more
clearly than you, and show you the straight path.

One word more. Never speak evil. May I tell
you, who love your country with all my heart, that
this has been the great fault here. During these last
eight years I have seen so many sorrows which
could have been avoided or lessened if a little word
had not been breathed here and there, perhaps
without evil intention, and thus destroyed the happiness or even the life of someone. Nurses all need
to think on this, and to cultivate a loyalty and team
spirit among themselves.

If any of you has a grievance against me, I beg
you to forgive me; I have perhaps been unjust
sometimes, but I have loved you much more than
you think.

I send my good wishes for the happiness of all
my girls, as much for those who have left the school
as for those who are still there. Thank you for the
kindness you have always shown me.

Your Matron,

EDITH CAVELL

For four years after her death she lay in an unobtrusive
grave in a corner of the *Tir National.* The Germans refused repeated requests for the return of her body for burial
in England, and so for that time she rested among the
Belgians whom she had loved, and served, so well. But in
May 1919, the war over at last, she came home. Not,

as she had done so often in the past, on the little cross-channel steamer, but with great ceremony, aboard H.M.S. *Rowena*. As the battleship entered Dover harbor every ship in sight lowered her flag. Her coffin, shrouded in the Union Jack, was carried ashore by sailors of the Royal Navy and borne in procession to the station, where it was placed in a purple-draped railway coach specially designed and built by the Southern Railway, and guarded throughout the night by soldiers.

Thousands of silent people lined the streets of London the next day as her funeral procession made its way to Westminster Abbey, where the Queen of England waited, among the highest dignitaries in the land, to pay a last tribute to the quiet, humble nurse about whom few had heard until — by one hasty, ill-considered action — the Germans had written her name across the sky in letters of fire.

At her family's request, Edith now sleeps in the shadow of the walls of Norwich Cathedral. She is back among the people from whom she sprang: at rest.

The memory of her life and work in Belgium is kept green in the splendid Edith Cavell – Marie Depage Institute in Brussels, and the model Nursing Service now flourishing in Belgium, which stands proudly beside the other nursing services of the world. Nor is she forgotten in the hospitals where she trained and worked in England. The London still bears the proud reputation of being one of the foremost training hospitals in the country. The North St. Pancras Infirmary — no longer a humble "Poor Law Institute" — is part of the Whittington Hospital, Highgate (and the window of what was Edith Cavell's room still looks out over gardens and parkland, as it did more than sixty years ago). Shoreditch Infirmary (now St. Leonard's, Hoxton) remembers her still, and still carries on its work among the people of London's East End.

Even the Fountain Hospital — that "temporary" building hastily erected during the fever epidemic of 1895 — still stands, and its pioneer work among mentally handicapped children, in which it leads the world, would have given Edith, with her great love of children, especial pleasure. Perhaps, even today, her friendly ghost walks the concrete paths and corrugated-iron wards, happy among the children who are learning to live a new, and better life among the devoted nurses who care for them.

In Manchester the windows of Bradford House still look out on the winding gear of a nearby coal mine, and the nurses who pass through its tall gates each day still slip on the sooty flagstones as they hurry along Ashton New Road and Gray Mare Lane on the way to see their patients. But the homes they enter are more comfortable now, and their patients better fed; just as there is less fear of the surgeon's knife and the doctor's little black bag everywhere than there was in Edith's day. The sight of an ambulance standing at the door is no longer one which sends whole streets of people into a frenzy of terror. To most, it is the symbol of hope, and not despair as it once was.

Had she lived, Edith Cavell would have seen many of these changes take place, and enjoyed something of the reward she earned during a lifetime of self-sacrifice and service. But if she had lived — and died as unobtrusively

— how many of us would remember her now? How many would have been spurred on by her example to serve as she served her fellow men?

There are times when only a discordant note can draw attention to the beauty of a great musical work; can startle listeners into an awareness of its majesty. Such a note was sounded in the early morning of October 12th, 1915, when a volley of gunfire rang out over the *Tir National* in Brussels, and ended a life which had been, in every way, an inspiration to those who follow.

ELIZABETH GREY lives with her husband, Garry Hogg, in a country house on the Kent-Sussex border in England. She gave up a commercial career to become a full-time writer, beginning with short stories and articles. Her first book was published in 1955 and has been followed by many others, ranging from career stories to travel books. *Friend Within the Gates* is her first historical biography and she regards it as her most important book to date. Each spring Elizabeth Grey and her husband make trips abroad to collect material for radio scripts, articles, and books. Whenever there is time for it they both enjoy reading, walking, listening to music, and interior decoration.